# *the* Mediterranean
# REFRESH
## Under 30 Minutes

# *the* Mediterranean
# REFRESH

## Under 30 Minutes

**FAST PREPPING** for Clean Eating

## VERONICA MILES

peapil

**peapil**

PEAPIL PUBLISHING
PO Box 65460
Salt Lake City, Utah 84165
www.peapil.com

*Interior by Ashley Tucker*
*Cover Design by Ashley Tucker*
*Contributions by Kirsten Armstrong*
*Photography by David E. Carranza Calvillo*
*Food Styling by Itze McConnehey*

First Edition

Contact the author at support@peapil.com

Paperback ISBN: 979-8-859394-85-2
Hardback ISBN: 978-1-990281-62-4
eBook ISBN: 978-1-990281-61-7
Audiobook ISBN: 978-1-990281-60-0

**Disclaimer**

All material on Peapil.com and in this book is provided for your information only and may not be construed as medical advice or instruction. No action or inaction should be taken based solely on the contents of this information; instead, readers should consult appropriate health professionals on any matter relating to their health and well-being. If you think you may have a medical emergency, call your doctor or 911 immediately.

The content of this book (text, graphics, and images) is not intended to be a substitute for professional medical advice, diagnosis, or treatment. Always seek the advice of your physician or other qualified health provider with any questions you may have regarding a medical condition.

Never disregard professional medical advice or delay in seeking it because of something you have read in this book. The information and opinions expressed here are believed to be accurate, based on the best judgment available to the authors. Readers who fail to consult with appropriate health authorities assume the risk of any injuries. Reliance on any information and content provided by Peapil Publishing and this book is solely at your own risk.

The publisher is not responsible for errors or omissions.

# CONTENTS

# Introduction

I was sixteen years old when I first saw the Mediterranean Sea. It stretched across the horizon, a mesmerizing cerulean blue. I didn't know it at the time, but that trip would completely change the course of my life.

Growing up, my parents had always said when I turned sixteen, they would send me to Greece. Both of them had grown up in Greece, but moved to America for more opportunities. The trip would be only the third time I ever saw my Nona, and I was craving an adventure.

This was decades ago, and while I've forgotten many of the details of my trip, I can still remember the *feeling*. In Greece—and the Mediterranean in general—I felt a sense of togetherness I had never experienced before. Strangers were friendly, families ate every meal together, and the community felt tightly woven together. It felt like home.

I also remember the food. Colorful dishes I had never seen before, fragrances I'd never smelled, and flavors I didn't know existed. I was eager to try as many things as possible. I wanted to soak in the sensuous experience of the Mediterranean. Honestly, I never wanted to go back to American cuisine, and truth be told, I never did. The trip gave me a new sense of direction, one that led me to culinary school and eventually back to the Mediterranean region.

As a new graduate, I felt ready to take on the world, so I flew back to the Mediterranean. The six years I spent there after culinary school only deepened the love and appreciation for the region. The spark that had begun with my trip to Greece quickly grew into a flame that led me to travel along the Mediterranean Sea, learning every aspect of the region's inspirational cuisine.

## Spain

I began in Spain—the world's largest producer of olive oil. Since olive oil is an integral part of the Mediterranean cuisine (more on that later), it felt like kismet. The key ingredients cooks use in Spain include garlic, herbs, chicken, lamb, and seafood. Most of their dishes use techniques like stewing, roasting, broiling, grilling, and baking. I lived in the house of a family friend on the coast. My hosts taught me that traditional Spanish food is simple and uncomplicated, with the ingredients usually grown on their own property.

## France

After a month, I moved on to France. I loved the small cottage houses lining the cobblestone roads. It almost felt like I had been transported back in time. Coastal French cuisine is a combination of two regional cuisines: Provençal and Occitan. Both involve lots of seafood, such as sardines, sea urchins, octopus, and small fish called *rouget* and *loup*. They also use lamb, chickpeas, cheese, olives, and olive oil. The flavors are usually quite strong and unique. As with Spanish cooking, the techniques are relatively simple … that is, until you get into their baking!

**DISH TO TRY:** *Bouillabaisse* (fish stew)

## Italy

I remember it was a hot July when I arrived in Italy. I rented a small apartment on the Amalfi Coast and hired a chef to come and teach me the local techniques. Thanks to its front-row access to the sea, Italy has historically had access to a wide variety of spices—all of which Italians use in their cooking! Italian cuisine revolves around olive oil, cheese, olives, garlic, tomatoes, fish, pasta, and bread. As I'm sure you can guess, boiling and simmering are common Italian cooking techniques. Meats are usually prepared through roasting and braising, however tough and flavorful cuts are sometimes cooked in hot water.

**DISH TO TRY:** *Focaccia* (flatbread)

## Greece

During my stint in Greece, I stayed with my Nona and spent the entire visit in her kitchen. The familiar smells and flavors brought me back to my sixteen-year-old self. It felt like all the pieces of my life were falling into place.

The key ingredients used in Greece include seafood, cheese, olive oil, lemons, vegetables, nuts, and lamb. There is an unspoken formula to Greek cooking—a base of roasted or stewed meat and/or vegetables wrapped in bread or pastry. Savory pies like these are staples in Greek cuisine, served whole or cut into triangles.

**DISH TO TRY:** *Spanakotyropita* (spinach and cheese pie)

## Turkey

Turkish food is part of the Ottoman cuisine. The key ingredients here include butter, olive oil, seafood, and spices. Ottoman food is primarily boiled and sautéed, and soups are a staple dish, commonly prepared with chicken stock, rice, and vegetables. Fun fact: years ago, an Ottoman garlic-flavored soup was sold as a hangover cure in the mornings.

I remember the first time I used a *çaydanlık*; a Turkish teapot with two tiers. The top tier steeps the tea, while the bottom boils the water. My entire experience in Turkey felt surreal. The stiff coastal breezes, sea turtles, and white sand are memories I'll cherish forever.

**DISH TO TRY:** *Piyaziye* (meat-stuffed onions)

## Egypt

It was October by the time I reached Egypt, and I was thankful for the warm weather. I'm used to colorful leaves dancing in the wind throughout October. Instead, in Egypt I spent the month soaking up the sun, while absorbing all I could about the local cuisine.

Most Egyptian meals incorporate rice and bread paired with vegetables. Since many Egyptians are vegetarian (either for religious reasons or due to the historically high price of meat), there is an emphasis on whole, fresh produce. Other common ingredients include cheese, legumes, fruits, lamb, and chicken. Dessert is very popular in Egypt, especially those made with dates, honey, almonds, and syrups.

**DISH TO TRY:** Kebab

## Libya and Morocco

Maghrebi cuisine encompasses the food traditions of Tunisia, Algeria, Libya, Morocco, and Mauritania. Thanks to all these influences, the food of this region features many diverse flavors.

Maghrebi cooking is usually comprised of seafood, goat, lamb, dates, nuts, legumes, and fresh produce. During my trip, I first stayed in Al Uqay-lah, Libya, a coastal city within the Gulf of Sidra. There I learned to cook in a traditional tajine over open flames, and used lots of spices, including ginger, cumin, cinnamon, turmeric, and saffron. I learned that sweet and sour is a popular combination when cooking with the tajine, especially lamb with prunes and seasoning.

By the time I moved on to my final stint in Morocco, I had already learned many of the most common Maghrebi techniques, so I decided to reward myself by spending the final weeks enjoying the warmth and con-templating how I could bring the lessons from my trip back home with me. I was young, but ambitious. I wanted to share my experiences with everyone, but I knew people wouldn't always be open to change. I've learned that "new" foods can intimidate people, which is why I'm thankful I visited Greece at a young age. I wanted to learn. I craved something different; and that's exactly what I got.

**DISH TO TRY:** Couscous with vegetables and meat

# What Is the Mediterranean Diet?

Put simply, the Mediterranean Diet is a way of eating that reflects the Mediterranean region. With its ever-changing terrain and coastal connections, the Mediterranean is a multifaceted region, and the Mediterranean Diet is influenced by nine different cuisines. While it incorporates a wide range of flavors and aromas, we can categorize the diet into four food groups; healthy fats, unrefined carbs, protein, and non-starchy vegetables. These are predominantly whole, unprocessed foods.

The Mediterranean Diet emphasizes a plant-based approach to eating, with fish, poultry, and dairy products in moderation, while avoiding red meat and processed foods. Olive oil is a main component of the diet, used as a replacement for butter in nearly all cooking and baking. Olive oil boasts many health benefits, such as fighting inflammation and boosting heart health!

A true Mediterranean meal bursts with color. The smells should entice you, and the flavors should wow you. The Mediterranean Diet flaunts dishes that are not only vibrantly beautiful, but also have many health benefits. Both of these advantages originate from the use of healthful, wholesome foods.

# Why Choose the Mediterranean Diet?

You may have heard that people from the Mediterranean live longer lives and boast healthier hearts. If so, you've heard right! A Mediterranean Diet can reduce your risk of all-cause death by around 25 percent.[1] If you're considered at high risk for cardiovascular disease, it can also lower your chances of a deadly cardiovascular event.[2] But the health benefits don't end there.

The Mediterranean Diet really is the first line of defense for many chronic illnesses. Thanks to the whole foods and lack of processed junk, the diet has been recommended by doctors everywhere for decades! So, what else can it do for you?

## Protects Against Certain Cancers

Researchers believe that the emphasis on fruits, vegetables, and whole grains is the reason behind the Mediterranean Diet's protective role against cancer. Specifically, a 2017 study found that the diet can reduce an individual's risk of breast and colorectal cancer.[3]

Interestingly, breast cancer cases have climbed 20 percent since 2008. And while that's a worrisome statistic, a simple diet change may have a positive effect on your own personal risk. Another study discovered a 62 percent lower risk of breast cancer in women who followed a Mediterranean Diet, compared to a low-fat diet.[4] The Mediterranean Diet they participated in focused heavily on extra-virgin olive oil as the primary source of fat.

## May Reduce Depression

Unfortunately, depression is a prevalent condition all over the world, but is especially concentrated in America. While therapy and medications can help mediate the condition, depression still makes life extremely difficult.

After reviewing forty-one studies, researchers found that the Mediterranean Diet may lower depression cases. When compared to a typical American diet, which is loaded with sugar, meat, and trans-fat, the Mediterranean Diet can actually reduce depression rates by 33 percent.[5] This provides depression sufferers a viable option that can be paired with their current treatments.

## May Encourage and Maintain Weight Loss

When it comes to weight loss, it's well known that the fastest option isn't always the best one. Most dieters who lose weight too quickly end up gaining it all back, along with additional pounds. If you're looking for a sustainable option, the Mediterranean Diet is it!

A 2015 study revealed the Mediterranean Diet to be more effective at weight loss than low-fat diets, with the Mediterranean Dieters losing between eight and twenty-two pounds in one year.[6] The same paper explained that not only did the diet benefit participants' weight, it also reduced their blood pressure and significantly improved the effects of type 2 diabetes.

## May Prevent Cognitive Decline

The ways in which the Mediterranean Diet benefits the heart can also have benefits for your brain! Issues with a person's vascular health (blood vessels) affect not only the heart, but also the brain. This is because blood vessels bring nutrients and oxygen to both organs. And when your diet supplies your blood vessels with essential nutrients and vitamins, you may see a decrease in cognitive decline.

In 2016, a review looked at eighteen studies and concluded that the Mediterranean Diet "was related to either slowing the rate of cognitive decline, minimizing the conversion to [Alzheimer's/dementia], or improving the cognitive function."[7] As with depression, a Mediterranean Diet will not cure these cognitive diseases, but it can prevent and reduce symptoms when paired with other treatments.

## May Prevent and Help Manage Type 2 Diabetes

After following over four hundred people without diabetes for four years, researchers discovered a 52 percent lower risk for developing the illness when following a Mediterranean Diet.[8] Simply, the diet was found to be inversely related to diabetes cases. What does this mean?

If you're at risk for developing diabetes, a Mediterranean Diet is a great option to reduce your chances of getting it. While other treatment options should be explored, supplementing your diet with the pillars of the Mediterranean Diet (think whole, fresh foods) can be a starting point.

# The Mediterranean Food Pyramid

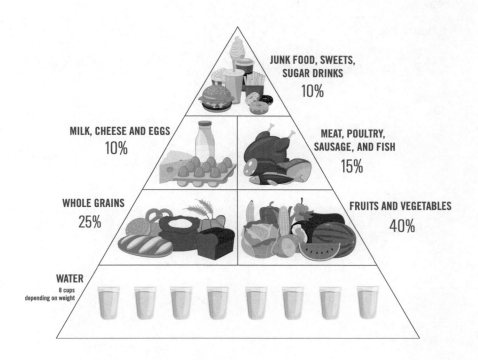

Now that you're familiar with the health benefits produced by the Mediterranean Diet, let's explore it in detail! This food pyramid was developed by the Mediterranean Diet Foundation Expert Group and shows which foods you should consume as part of the Mediterranean lifestyle. Each recipe in this book closely follows this pyramid. Here you can find the basic percentages of each food group that should make up your daily diet, based on the Mediterranean Food Pyramid:

| | |
|---|---|
| Water | 7–8 (8-oz.) cups a day |
| Fresh Fruits and Vegetables | 40% • Opt for fresh, seasonal fruits and veggies. If you're ever hungry, you can always eat more veggies! |
| Whole Grains | 25% |
| Meat, Poultry, and Fish | 15% • Always choose poultry or fish over red meat. If serving red meat, make portions small. |
| Dairy Products | 10% |
| Junk Food and Sweets | 10% |

# Food Groups

As mentioned earlier, the Mediterranean Diet highlights four key food groups; healthy fats, unrefined carbs, protein, and non-starchy vegetables. The foods you see in the Mediterranean Food Pyramid fall into these food groups seamlessly.

## Healthy Fats

When you think of the Mediterranean Diet, I bet your mind goes to olive oil, avocados, and nuts, right? Guess what all those have in common—they're healthy fats! When it comes to fat, one size doesn't fit all. There are actually three types, and while two should be avoided, the other one is "healthy" and quite important to our wellbeing.

The two types of fat we should avoid are saturated fat and trans-fat. Both have been shown to harm your health by causing inflammation, increasing bad cholesterol levels, and increasing the risk of heart disease. Saturated fats are found in meats, dark poultry, butter, cheese, and coconut oil. Trans-fats are found in fried foods, margarine, baked goods, and processed foods. Saturated fats should be eaten in moderation, but trans-fat should be avoided at all costs.

The Mediterranean Diet focuses on "healthy" fats, also known as unsaturated fats. Two common subtypes of unsaturated fat are monounsaturated and Polyunsaturated fats. They are usually found in plant-based foods such as vegetables, nuts, and seeds.

Foods with high concentrations of monounsaturated fats include olive oil, avocados, nuts, and peanut butter. Polyunsaturated fats are found in seeds, walnuts, fatty fish, tofu, and soy milk. Both these fats boost heart health and lower bad cholesterol levels, while increasing good cholesterol levels. They also fight inflammation!

While unsaturated fat boosts our health, it also adds flavor and texture to our recipes. Fat can amplify the flavors of a dish, but also contributes its own flavor. For example, olive oil does not cover up the flavor of a dish, instead it enhances and adds to it. Fat creates five distinct textures in food; creamy, light, tender, flaky, and crisp. Without fat, food would be much more boring with a lot less flavor.

Olive oil is a very common fat in Mediterranean recipes—arguably the most common. I always suggest using extra-virgin olive oil because it is the least processed. If you're deciding which olive oil to purchase, try tasting it. If you can still feel the oil in your mouth minutes after, it's a sign of high quality.

While we're usually told to avoid it, fat is not the enemy;.it's a friend! Don't shy away from it because of misinformation. Healthy fats make up an entire category within the Mediterranean Diet for a reason!

## Healthy fats to keep in your kitchen:

- Olives and olive oil
- Nut or seed oils (canola, soybean, flaxseed oil)
- Nuts and nut butters (peanut butter, almond butter)

- Avocados
- Fatty fish (fresh tuna, salmon, sardines, trout, herring)
- Seeds
- Eggs

- Dark chocolate
- Tofu
- Yogurt

## Unrefined Carbs

The difference between refined and unrefined carbs is simple; refined carbs are processed, while unrefined are not. The Mediterranean Diet focuses solely on unrefined carbs, which contain naturally occurring fiber. In refined carbs, the fiber has usually been removed or changed in some way.

Unrefined carbs include whole-wheat or multigrain breads, quinoa, brown rice, oats, strawberries, and apples. Refined carbs include bagels, pastries, waffles, white rice, and white-flour bread.

While your brain may find refined carbs tempting, your body disagrees. When you eat refined carbs, your bloodstream is flooded with sugar, which turns to glucose. And while we need glucose for energy, too much of it turns into stored fat. When this sugar is released, our body creates insulin to clear it away. When this happens, the insulin creates a strong sense of hunger and usually leads to cravings, which can also lead to weight gain.

The reason we tend to gravitate toward refined carbs is because they're loaded with sugar, which makes them taste good. It's important to remember that eating a few refined carbs will not hurt you! Just try to limit your intake. For example, if you're at a restaurant and white bread is your only option, that's okay, but try not to eat it every day.

Some people worry that when they cut back on refined carbs, they'll experience intense cravings or feel unsatisfied. This is not true—you can feel satisfied with unrefined carbs. When you eat unrefined carbs, you not only reduce your sugar intake, you also prevent a spike in blood sugar. This will actually lead to less cravings! And your food will digest more slowly thanks to the extra fiber, meaning you'll feel fuller for longer. Really, there are many benefits to choosing unrefined carbs over refined ones.

I'll be honest, it may be difficult to transition to the Mediterranean Diet if you're used to mostly eating refined carbs. If that's the case, take your time to make the transition. You don't need to flip your entire diet overnight. Take a few weeks to reduce refined carbs and slowly switch to unrefined carbs. Your body will thank you!

## Unrefined carbs to keep in your kitchen:

- Whole-wheat or multigrain bread
- Quinoa
- Brown rice
- Barley
- Nuts
- Legumes (kidney beans, lentils, peas)
- Vegetables (spinach, green beans, tomatoes, celery)
- Fruits (apples, berries, bananas, pears)

# Protein

When I think about protein, my mind goes straight to meat, and while meat does offer high amounts of protein, it's *not* the only option. Focusing on meat may even limit your protein intake overall, since meat usually isn't eaten with each meal.

Why do we even need protein? Well, it allows our bodies to grow and repair themselves. Every single cell in the human body has protein. The basic structure of protein is a chain of amino acids. Amino acids are used to create new proteins, which help with bone and muscle growth. They are also harnessed for energy and hormone production.

In total, there are about twenty different amino acids. Your body can make eleven of them, which are considered nonessential. The nine your body cannot make are known as essential amino acids. You require both types for your body to function properly.

The recommended daily intake of protein varies based on age, gender, weight, and health concerns. However, most adult women need between 50 and 60 grams of protein a day, while most men require 55 to 70 grams of protein.

There are many food options that can help you achieve these protein requirements. Within the Mediterranean Diet, common protein-rich foods include fish, chicken, tofu, nuts, seeds, legumes, beans, Greek yogurt, and cheese. Per serving, the amount of protein fluctuates depending on the food. This variation is reflected in the chart below:

| FOOD | PROTEIN PER 100G |
|---|---|
| Salmon | 20g |
| Chicken | 27g |
| Tofu | 8g |
| Almonds | 21g |
| Chia seeds | 17g |
| Chickpeas | 19g |
| Greek yogurt | 10g |
| Cheddar cheese | 25g |

This chart is meant for comparison purposes only. Obviously, it is not recommended to eat 100 grams of almonds at once. However, if you struggle with meeting your daily protein goal, try sprinkling seeds or nuts into your meals. For example, chia seeds don't have much flavor, but are loaded with protein. Sprinkle them into your smoothies, yogurt, pudding, or even pasta sauce. Grab a handful of nuts when you're in a rush, or try adding a legume into one meal each day. Amino acids are the building blocks of your cells, so use your imagination and the recipes in this book to achieve your daily protein intake.

## Proteins to keep in your kitchen:

- Fish
- Seafood
- Eggs
- Soy products
- Legumes (beans, lentils, peas)
- Greek yogurt
- Tofu
- Nuts and seeds
- Cheeses

## Non-Starchy Vegetables

I know, I know … you're tired of hearing "eat more vegetables," but here we are. And while getting enough vegetables is important, it's worth noting that there are two types: starchy and non-starchy.

Higher amounts of starch, which is a type of carbohydrate, are found in starchy vegetables. Starch is considered a complex carb, meaning it is made up of intricate groupings of sugar molecules. Starch maintains its fiber content, fueling your body when it requires energy.

Starch is not only found in vegetables, but also in many other foods, such as oatmeal, cereal, whole-wheat bread, rice, pasta, quinoa, and bananas.

Starchy vegetables include beans, corn, chickpeas, lentils, peas, sweet potatoes, pumpkin, and zucchini. Non-starchy vegetables include spinach, broccoli, carrots, onions, tomatoes, cucumbers, and mushrooms. Some fruits are also considered non-starchy, such as raspberries, blueberries, lemons, and peaches.

The recommended daily intake of vegetables is 2½ cups. Experts suggest you meet this requirement with a mixture of both starchy and non-starchy vegetables. However, compared to starchy vegetables, non-starchy vegetables usually have far fewer calories per serving. For example, 100 grams of beans has 367 calories, while 100 grams of spinach contains 23 calories.

Because of this stark difference between the two vegetable types, the Mediterranean Diet suggests unlimited amounts of non-starchy vegetables. This keeps your calorie count low, while still helping you gain various nutrients!

Don't shy away from starchy vegetables completely, though, just because they're higher in calories. These vegetables offer many important nutrients that your body needs, especially fiber.

Interestingly, starchy foods are usually paired with calorie-dense foods. For example, whole-grain pasta is usually covered in a rich sauce, which may cause weight gain. If you're concerned about your calorie intake, try pairing starchy foods and vegetables with low-calorie foods, such as hummus (made from chickpeas) with carrots.

Remember, our bodies and minds need all kinds of food. Do not restrict yourself from anything. Enjoy your meals and ensure you're meeting your daily recommended intake of vegetables. If you're feeling snackish, nibble on some non-starchy vegetables!

## Non-starchy produce to keep in your kitchen:

- Greens (lettuce, spinach, cabbage, kale)
- Broccoli and cauliflower
- Carrots
- Onions
- Tomatoes
- Cucumbers
- Mushrooms
- Bell peppers
- Asparagus
- Berries
- Melons
- Figs
- Citrus fruits

# Foods to Avoid

## Fast Food

A report published by the National Health and Nutrition Examination Survey claims that 36.6 percent of Americans, or about 85 million adults, consume fast food *every day* in the United States.[9] Every day!

At its core, fast food is calorie-dense, loaded with sodium, and filled with "bad" fats. The classic Big Mac contains 44 percent of our daily sodium intake and 53 percent of our daily saturated fat intake. Too much saturated fat and sodium are linked to increased risks of cardiovascular disease and stroke. Adding a medium order of fries tacks on another 11 percent in both categories. Just *one* simple meal at McDonald's puts us well over half the recommended intake for saturated fats and sodium. And there are still two more meals left in the day! Additionally, just a burger and fries contains almost 900 calories. Throw in ketchup packets, a large soda, and maybe even a soft-serve ice cream, and it's no surprise that fast food is the leading cause of obesity.

## Red Meat

Burgers, ribs, steak, sausage. What do they all have in common? They're all juicy, tasty, tender—and, as it turns out, poor for our health.

Studies have shown that people who consume a large amount of red meat increase their risk of dying from various causes. Two surveys monitored the red meat intake of over 100,000 participants for thirty-two years. During this research period, close to 24,000 subjects passed away from numerous causes, but most significantly owing to cardiovascular disease (5,900 people) and cancer (9,500 people). When taking into consideration outside influences and risk factors, the study concluded that with each additional serving of red meat, the risk of general death increased by 13 percent.[10]

## Processed Foods and Sweets

It's surprising how much of the food North Americans eat on a regular basis is processed. Everything from packaged bread, breakfast cereals, and frozen pizzas to instant noodles and packaged sandwich meats are "processed foods," meaning they've been chemically altered to prolong their shelf life, to make them taste better, or look more appealing. As I'm sure you've figured out by now, these foods can be quite detrimental to our health.

Just like fast food, processed foods are high in both saturated and trans-fats, not to mention sodium, added sugars, and empty calories. Trans and saturated fats are strongly linked to an increased risk of cardiovascular disease and stroke. Processed foods provide instant satisfaction by quenching hunger and offering a slight boost in energy, but those short-term effects hide long-term ramifications. One study with close to 20,000 participants claimed that for "each additional serving of ultra-processed food, all-cause mortality increased by 18%."[11]

I'm not trying to terrify you with appalling stats on the dangers of the traditional American diet, or to shame anybody for eating unhealthily. There's nothing wrong with occasionally splurging or enjoying processed food, as long as it's in moderation. Occasional exceptions are fine and are even beneficial for our mental health! But to fully understand the benefits of the Mediterranean lifestyle, we have to realize the current North American diet is failing its followers.

# Mediterranean Principles

We've covered what puts the Mediterranean Diet ahead of others nutrition-ally, but the food you eat is just one aspect of a diet. While wholesome foods are the pillar of a healthy diet, so is eating in moderation and mindfully. As with all cultures, the Mediterranean region has its own outlook on food— one that is different from the relationship most Americans have with food. When transitioning to a Mediterranean Diet, it's important to also embrace the region's eating principles, so you can enhance your experience and your results.

## Eating in Moderation

This is something we're reminded of again and again, but what exactly does eating in moderation mean? It means eating as much food as your body needs. It's important to listen to your body and to stop eating when you're full, but not uncomfortable.

There are a few tips that can help with this Mediterranean principle. First, don't completely eliminate any foods. The more foods you ban, the more likely you are to binge. Instead, portion out reasonable servings. As you gradually reduce the amount of food you eat, you'll find you don't crave it as much anymore.

As I'm sure you've noticed, serving sizes in restaurants have dramatically increased over the last few decades. Sadly, this has nothing to do with people's appetites; it has more to do with common patterns of overeating.

In the Mediterranean, meals are rarely served for one; they are usually eaten with loved ones. Eating together is a bonding experience that helps to connect people and create a touchpoint for their days. Another benefit of eating together, though, is that it encourages eating in moderation. The more you speak and listen, the slower you eat. This gives your stomach a chance to catch up on all the digesting and register how much you've eaten. When you eat quickly, your stomach doesn't have the time to communicate fullness, which can lead to overeating, bloating, and stomach pain.

If you're unable to dine with others, I'd suggest finding other ways to slow down your eating. Engage with the meal in some way; try counting your bites or asking yourself what parts of the dish you enjoy. Immersing yourself in your food is a very common and healthy Mediterranean practice.

I find that eating in moderation comes down to how your view food. For the people of the Mediterranean, food is seen as nourishment and an experience, not just as fuel to get them through their daily activities. Find time to slow down between your life events to truly enjoy the experience of food.

## Seasonal Foods

Throughout much of history, humans have relied on the seasons to dictate our food choices. Spring brings us spinach, carrots, and asparagus. Summer harvests include apples, corn, and cucumbers, while autumn includes squashes, beets, and figs.

Due to the development of our complex food distribution system, we can now eat most foods whenever we want. And while this may seem convenient, there are a few reasons to consider prioritizing seasonal foods.

First, seasonal produce simply tastes better. Mass-produced foods are grown to meet quantity standards, not quality standards, which is why your homegrown veggies always taste better. Because of the ridiculously high demand for produce, flavor just isn't much of a concern for most large-scale growers. In fact, a 2016 study found that shelf life and appearance were prioritized over taste.[12]

Seasonal produce is also much better for the environment. At the grocery store we don't always consider where our foods come from, but think about it for a minute: Did your wintertime bell peppers and tomatoes come from your home state, or were they flown in from Mexico? Consider the difference in emissions. Consider the environmental impact.

Ever wonder why most produce prices climb in winter? It's all due to availability. When most domestic produce is limited in the colder months, we rely on imports from warmer countries. Over one-third of U.S. produce is imported,[13] mostly because year-round demand conflicts with seasonal growing cycles.

If you prioritize recipes that favor in-season produce, you'll notice an improvement in taste and a decrease in prices. Personally, I appreciate produce more when it's less available. If I can always snack on cherry tomatoes, I just don't get excited about them anymore. But if they are only in season for a month or so, I really savor my one chance to experience them. Obviously if you're in need of an out-of-season food, don't restrict yourself. It's about being mindful of your choices, not limiting them.

So, how can you shop seasonally?

First stop: your local farmers' market. Get to know the farmers and what produce they offer during each season. You can also look into joining a CSA (community-supported agriculture) program with a simple Google search. Because available produce differs between states, I won't include a list of seasonal foods here. Instead, I suggest you take some time to discover what grows when in your community.

## Spices and Herbs

How can you take a simple dish and elevate it in seconds? Spices and herbs. This is a trick Mediterranean people have kept in their back pocket for centuries. Spices and herbs enhance any food or drink by providing flavor, color, and fragrance, adding an incomparable nuance.

You may be wondering what the difference is between spices and herbs. While there is a bit of debate on concrete definitions, I consider an herb the whole or part of a plant, usually fresh, that is used to flavor food. A spice is derived from a dried plant, such as a seed or bark, which is usually ground up and used to flavor food. An example to visualize the difference is that ground cinnamon is a spice made from bark, while a basil leaf is considered an herb.

As you transition to Mediterranean foods, you'll find that quality spices and herbs are an integral part of the diet. I always suggest spending the extra few bucks for fresh, high-quality options, because trust me, there really is a difference.

High-quality spices and herbs will have a distinctive and strong aroma. If you find the smell overwhelming, the spice is probably very fresh; this will fade over time. Another option is to make spices and grow herbs yourself. While it takes some extra effort, I find the process of drying homegrown herbs and grinding them up to be satisfying and almost meditative!

Another tip is to purchase whole spices and grind them yourself as needed. They stay fresher for longer this way, and are more likely to retain full potency. Instead of buying premixed spice blends, consider making your own. It's super easy and very quick—just grab a few mason jars and get mixing.

To perk up your spices, toast them in a skillet for about one minute before adding to your recipe. This allows the spice to fully release its aroma. If your recipe calls for cooking with some sort of heat, that's when you should add in any dried spices. As for fresh herbs, leave them for last. If they take on too much heat, they'll lose their flavor.

To get your kitchen ready for Mediterranean dishes, below is a list of some of the most common Mediterranean spices and herbs. If you're not growing your own herbs, you don't need to stock up on them—just purchase whatever your recipe calls for during your regular grocery trip. Since high-quality whole spices can last up to five years, I suggest purchasing them slowly over time to build an entire collection. I've starred the most common Mediterranean spices below, so you can start with these:

| | | |
|---|---|---|
| • Basil | • Dill | • Paprika |
| • Bay leaves | • Fennel | • Rosemary |
| • Black pepper | • Garlic powder | • Saffron |
| • Cilantro | • Ginger | • Sage |
| • Cloves | • Mint | • Sumac |
| • Coriander | • Oregano | • Thyme |
| • Cumin | • Parsley | • Turmeric |

## Plate Math

If you look at any Mediterranean dish, you should see that about half the plate is vegetables and fruits. That, my friends, is plate math! If you despise math, don't worry—plate math is different. Essentially, it's all about visualizing what a healthy balance should look like on the plate.

Following the Mediterranean food pyramid, each meal should be broken down into fractions based on the type of food you're eating. For example, a perfectly balanced dish would have:

65% carbs (40% fruits and vegetables and 25% whole grains), 15% protein (focusing on poultry, seafood, and fish), and 20% healthy fats.

How do you make sure you're following those guidelines? This is where plate math comes in. To simplify the percentages mentioned above, I like to think about my plate being divided into five portions (each representing 20 percent of the total meal). Each meal should have:

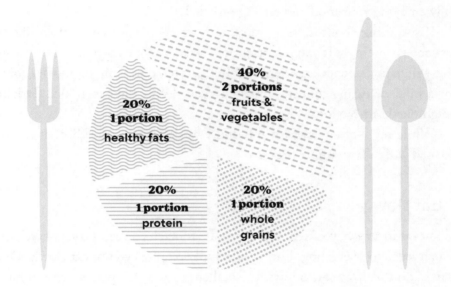

Since we've already discussed which foods go in each of these groups, hopefully you can imagine what a meal broken down this way would look like. An example would be Mackerel & Tomato Spaghetti (page 230).

Of course, the exact percentages will vary depending on the meal. Sometimes your dinner may have a bit more protein, while your breakfast may have more carbs, and that's okay. For example, if you're eating a salad, you're less likely to get your portion of whole grains. But as long as your salad is high in fiber (think nuts, beans, and artichoke hearts), it's completely fine—remember, the whole reason we want whole grains is for the fiber! There's always room to play around.

I'd like to make something clear: there are no hard and fast rules with any diet. Plate math is only meant to help you *visualize* the necessary food groups. If you find it restrictive or confusing, skip it! What works for me won't work for everyone, but I wanted to share this principle.

## Mindful Eating

People from the Mediterranean are less likely to experience disordered eating than Americans, not only because of *what* they eat, but also because of *how* they eat. As I mentioned earlier, mindful eating is an integral part of fully enjoying your food and feeling satisfied.

If you think about it, being mindful is an approach that is applicable to just about anything. If you pay attention, you're more engaged, and therefore you will gain a deeper experience. Whether you're watching a movie, going for a hike, or eating dinner, immersing yourself in the experience leads to heightened satisfaction.

While most of us don't eat mindfully by default, it is a skill that can be learned with a few simple tricks:

## 1. Eat slowly

If you eat in a rush, you're not giving your stomach enough time to catch up, which leads to overeating. Eating mindfully requires you to eat slowly. One way to do this is by starting with a smaller portion. Try placing your utensil down between bites to prevent yourself from rushing. If you're prone to speed eating when you're starving, I suggest grazing throughout the day whenever you're feeling snackish. This will help you prevent binge eating and encourage mindful eating.

## 2. Engage all your senses

Do you usually flick on the television or open your Facebook feed when you sit down to a meal? If so, you're definitely not eating mindfully. Remove the distractions and engage your senses. How does your food taste? What do you enjoy about it? What does it smell and look like? What colors stand out? Use your senses to reflect on your meal. As you chew, try to identify the ingredients you cooked with. Are you experiencing that sprinkle of oregano?

### 3. Take small bites

Taking small bites allows you to experience the food better. When you over-load your fork and mouth, you're more eager to swallow than enjoy it. Take small bites and chew your food thoroughly: A good rule of thumb is thirty chews before swallowing. This also gives your mouth a chance to start the digestion process, making it easier on your stomach!

### 4. Appreciate your food

Instead of sitting down to a meal and digging in right away, take time to appreciate your food. Consider the effort it took to cook the meal and to prepare the ingredients. Give yourself a few minutes to practice gratitude before taking your first bite.

### 5. Grocery shop with a list

Mindful eating doesn't start and end in the kitchen! Before you go out gro-cery shopping, ensure you're prepared with a list. This will help you to stay focused and prevent you from purchasing unneeded convenient foods. Fill your cart with produce, proteins, and whole grains, most of which are usually found around the perimeter of the store. Avoid the center aisles, unless you need to go there for a specific item on your list.

# 30-Minute Mediterranean Diet Recipes

I wanted to create a cookbook that encompassed quick and simple recipes. Whether you're a full-time worker, a sleep-deprived new mom, or busy with extracurricular activities, this cookbook was made for you!

The Mediterranean Diet may seem intimidating when you first transition to it—the shopping cart overflowing with produce usually does the trick. But once you start making these recipes, you'll realize the diet is for everyone, even those short on time.

Personally, what I truly love about this diet is how versatile it is! If you're vegetarian, vegan, gluten-free, or have other dietary restrictions, substitutions are a breeze.

Before you jump into these recipes, I want to thank you for supporting my journey! I hope you enjoy these dishes and share them with your loved ones. Remember, making this a sustainable change is going to take time. Immerse yourself in the experience and one day you'll look up and realize that Mediterranean cuisine has become your new diet.

## ALLERGENS

DF = Dairy Free

EF = Egg Free

GF = Gluten Free

NF = Nut Free

SF = Sugar Free

VE = Vegetarian

VG = Vegan

# BREAKFAST

**GF**
**SF**
**NF**

# Tangy Tuna Sandwich

**Servings: 3**

**PREP TIME:** 10 minutes | **COOK TIME:** 0 minutes | **TOTAL TIME:** 10 minutes

Level 1: Very Easy

This speedy Tangy Tuna Sandwich is a delicious way to start your day. If your mornings are *rushed*, try whipping this up the night before—it allows the flavors to really meld. Thanks to the apples and pickles, this meal offers a satisfying crunch!

## INGREDIENTS:

2 (5-oz.) cans tuna in oil, drained

5 pickles, thinly sliced

½ apple, thinly sliced

½ cup light mayonnaise

¼ cup fresh cilantro, chopped

3 tablespoons thinly sliced chives

1 tablespoon Dijon mustard

1 tablespoon unsalted butter

6 slices gluten-free bread, toasted

1 medium tomato, sliced

½ cucumber, sliced

## INSTRUCTIONS:

1. Combine the tuna, pickles, apple, mayonnaise, cilantro, chives, and Dijon mustard in a medium bowl, mixing well, until thoroughly combined.

2. Spread the butter onto the toasted bread slices and top three with the tuna mixture, tomato slices, and cucumber slices. Finish by placing the remaining buttered slices on top and serve.

| NUTRITION · per one serving · % of Daily Value | | | | | |
|---|---|---|---|---|---|
| Calories | 320 | — | Dietary Fiber | 5 g | 18% |
| Total Fat | 12 g | 15% | Total Sugars | 5 g | — |
| Saturated Fat | 3.1 g | 18% | Protein | 27 g | 54% |
| Polyunsaturated Fat | 5.1 g | — | Vitamin A | 208 mcg | 25% |
| Monounsaturated Fat | 2.8 g | — | Vitamin C | 11.2 mg | 10% |
| *Trans* Fat | — | — | Vitamin D | 1.4 mcg | 6% |
| Cholesterol | 40 mg | 13% | Potassium | 568 mg | 10% |
| Sodium | 450 mg | 20% | Calcium | 102 mg | 8% |
| Total Carbohydrates | 27 g | 10% | Iron | 3.8 mg | 20% |

GF
VE
NF
EF

# Strawberry Rhubarb Smoothie

**Servings: 1**

**PREP TIME:** 5 minutes | **COOK TIME:** 5 minutes | **TOTAL TIME:** 10 minutes

Level 1: Very Easy

In my family, smoothies reign as king of breakfasts! They're quick, convenient, and delicious—*what* more could you want? While strawberries are a fan favorite, I wanted to experiment with rhubarb since we grow it fresh in our garden. The result? The liquid version of strawberry–rhubarb pie, loaded with antioxidants and vitamins.

## INGREDIENTS:

1 cup water

1 rhubarb stalk, chopped

1 cup halved fresh strawberries

½ cup Greek yogurt

2 tablespoons raw honey

⅛ teaspoon ground cinnamon

3 ice cubes

## INSTRUCTIONS:

1. Heat the water in a small saucepan over medium-high heat. Let the water come to a boil, then add the rhubarb and cook it for 3 minutes, until tender, stirring occasionally. Drain the rhubarb.

2. Place the rhubarb in a blender along with the strawberries, yogurt, honey, and cinnamon, and blend until smooth.

3. Add the ice and blend once more, until it is thick and smooth. Serve and enjoy!

| NUTRITION · per one serving · % of Daily Value | | | | | |
|---|---|---|---|---|---|
| Calories | 220 | | Dietary Fiber | 4 g | 14% |
| Total Fat | 0.5 g | 1% | Total Sugars | 11 g | — |
| Saturated Fat | 0.1 g | 1% | Protein | 6 g | 12% |
| Polyunsaturated Fat | 0.2 g | — | Vitamin A | 21.5 mcg | 2% |
| Monounsaturated Fat | 0.1 g | — | Vitamin C | 88.8 mg | 100% |
| *Trans* Fat | — | — | Vitamin D | — | — |
| Cholesterol | 5 mg | 1% | Potassium | 443 mg | 10% |
| Sodium | 10 mg | — | Calcium | 125 mg | 10% |
| Total Carbohydrates | 21 g | 8% | Iron | 0.8 mg | 0.4% |

# Pistachio & Grape Yogurt Bowl

**Servings: 4**

**PREP TIME:** 5 minutes | **COOK TIME:** 0 minutes | **TOTAL TIME:** 5 minutes

Level 1: Very Easy

Nutty, subtly sweet pistachios, juicy grapes, and bright lemon juice may be a surprising combination, but when blended together they pack a flavorful punch! Chock-full of protein, minerals, and *fiber*, this is a winning *breakfast* combination. I always keep a few labeled mason jars full of various chopped nuts on hand to speed up my mornings.

## INGREDIENTS:

3 cups purple grapes

2 cups whole-fat or 2% Greek yogurt

¼ cup chopped pistachios

¼ cup chopped fresh mint

¼ cup honey

Juice of ½ lemon

2 tablespoons granola

2 tablespoons chopped walnuts

## INSTRUCTIONS:

1. Combine the grapes, yogurt, pistachios, mint, honey, and lemon juice in a food processor or blender and mix until smooth.

2. Divide the mixture among four serving cups or dishes and garnish with walnuts and granola, if desired.

| NUTRITION · per one serving · % of Daily Value | | | | | |
|---|---|---|---|---|---|
| Calories | 150 | | Dietary Fiber | 2 g | 7% |
| Total Fat | 3 g | 4% | Total Sugars | 8 g | — |
| Saturated Fat | 0.4 g | 2% | Protein | 10 g | 20% |
| Polyunsaturated Fat | 0.9 g | — | Vitamin A | 48 mcg | 6% |
| Monounsaturated Fat | 1.5 g | — | Vitamin C | 3.5 mg | 4% |
| *Trans* Fat | — | — | Vitamin D | — | — |
| Cholesterol | 5 mg | 1% | Potassium | 327 mg | 6% |
| Sodium | 30 mg | 1% | Calcium | 102 mg | 8% |
| Total Carbohydrates | 23 g | 8% | Iron | 0.7 mg | 4% |

# Walnut Date Shake

**Servings: 2**

**PREP TIME:** 5 minutes | **COOK TIME:** 0 minutes | **TOTAL TIME:** 10 minutes

Level 1: Very Easy

Date shakes have grown in popularity recently, especially within the state of California, but the fruit has belonged to the *Mediterranean* Diet for centuries! Packed with fiber and antioxidants, dates add a subtly sweet caramel flavor to this recipe, complemented by the crunchy walnuts.

## INGREDIENTS:

2 cups plain Greek yogurt

½ cup 2% milk

½ cup chopped walnuts

4 dates, pitted

2–3 ice cubes

½ teaspoon ground cinnamon

½ teaspoon vanilla extract

## INSTRUCTIONS:

1. Combine the yogurt, milk, walnuts, dates, ice cubes, cinnamon, and vanilla extract in a blender and mix until smooth and creamy.

2. Pour the mixture into two serving cups or dishes and serve.

**NUTRITION** · per one serving · % of Daily Value

| | | | | | |
|---|---|---|---|---|---|
| Calories | 420 | | Dietary Fiber | 4 g | 14% |
| Total Fat | 16 g | 21% | Total Sugars | 27g | — |
| Saturated Fat | 5.5 g | 28% | Protein | 15 g | 30% |
| Polyunsaturated Fat | 6.7 g | — | Vitamin A | 120 mcg | 15% |
| Monounsaturated Fat | 3.4 g | — | Vitamin C | 1.5 mg | 2% |
| *Trans* Fat | — | — | Vitamin D | 0.2 mcg | — |
| Cholesterol | 30 mg | 10% | Potassium | 803 mg | 15% |
| Sodium | 80 mg | 3% | Calcium | 415 mg | 30% |
| Total Carbohydrates | 34 g | 12% | Iron | 1.1 mg | 6% |

# Mediterranean Beet Smoothie

**Servings: 2**

**PREP TIME:** 5 minutes I **COOK TIME:** 0 minutes I **TOTAL TIME:** 5 minutes

Level 1: Very Easy

If you don't have an affinity for beets, don't turn the page just yet. Like their carrot and sweet potato cousins, beets offer a natural sweetness that enhances any smoothie. They're paired with mango and spinach here for a recipe that boasts iron, fiber, and vitamin C!

## INGREDIENTS:

2 cups loosely packed baby spinach

1 banana, sliced and frozen

1 small mango, sliced

6 ice cubes

1 teaspoon minced fresh ginger root

½ cup beet juice

½ cup unsweetened almond milk

## INSTRUCTIONS:

1. Combine the spinach, banana, mango, ice cubes, ginger root, beet juice, and milk in a blender and mix until smooth and creamy.

2. Pour the mixture into two serving cups or dishes and serve.

| NUTRITION · per one serving · % of Daily Value | | | | | |
|---|---|---|---|---|---|
| Calories | 180 | | Dietary Fiber | 5 g | 18% |
| Total Fat | 1 g | 1% | Total Sugars | 13 g | — |
| Saturated Fat | 0.2 g | 1% | Protein | 6 g | 12% |
| Polyunsaturated Fat | 0.1 g | — | Vitamin A | 1221 mcg | 140% |
| Monounsaturated Fat | 0.1 g | — | Vitamin C | 52 mg | 60% |
| Trans Fat | — | — | Vitamin D | 0.7 mcg | 4% |
| Cholesterol | — | — | Potassium | 753 mg | 15% |
| Sodium | 40 mg | 2% | Calcium | 119 mg | 10% |
| Total Carbohydrates | 31 g | 11% | Iron | 1.4 mg | 8% |

GF
VG
EF
DF

# Chocolate Quinoa Bowl

**Servings: 2**

**PREP TIME:** 5 minutes | **COOK TIME:** 10 minutes | **TOTAL TIME:** 15 minutes
Level 2: Easy

What's better than starting your day with chocolate? In this brownie-esque bowl, protein-packed quinoa is flavored with cocoa and then enriched with juicy berries, sweet maple syrup, and earthy cinnamon. Treat your body right and try out this energizing breakfast recipe!

## INGREDIENTS:

1½ cups quinoa, rinsed and drained

1½ cups water

1 cup unsweetened almond milk

2 tablespoons maple syrup

½ teaspoon vanilla extract

½ tablespoon unsweetened cocoa powder

¼ teaspoon ground cinnamon

¼ teaspoon salt

¼ cup fresh berries

½ banana, sliced

2 ounces dairy-free dark chocolate chips

## INSTRUCTIONS:

1. Coat your Instant Pot with nonstick cooking spray. Combine the quinoa, water, almond milk, maple syrup, vanilla extract, cocoa powder, cinnamon, and salt in the Instant Pot. Stir thoroughly, until well combined.

2. Set the Instant Pot to non-venting, seal it with the lid, and cook on high for 1 minute.

3. Switch the Instant Pot to venting and allow the pressure to release naturally for 10 minutes, then switch to the quick-release function.

4. Remove the lid and fluff the chocolate quinoa with a fork. Divide between two serving bowls and top with the berries, banana, and dark chocolate.

**NUTRITION** · per one serving · % of Daily Value

| | | | | | |
|---|---|---|---|---|---|
| Calories | 530 | | Dietary Fiber | 10 g | 36% |
| Total Fat | 8 g | 10% | Total Sugars | 12 g | — |
| Saturated Fat | 1 g | 5% | Protein | 19 g | 38% |
| Polyunsaturated Fat | 4.3 g | — | Vitamin A | 43.2 mcg | 4% |
| Monounsaturated Fat | 2.4 g | — | Vitamin C | 2.7 mg | 4% |
| Trans Fat | — | — | Vitamin D | 0.6 mcg | 4% |
| Cholesterol | — | — | Potassium | 842 mg | 20% |
| Sodium | 290 mg | 13% | Calcium | 216 mg | 15% |
| Total Carbohydrates | 95 g | 35% | Iron | 6.4 mg | 35% |

# Cauliflower & Egg Salad

**Servings: 4**

**PREP TIME:** 5 minutes | **COOK TIME:** 15 minutes | **TOTAL TIME:** 20 minutes

Level 3: Moderate

This low-carb alternative to potato salad keeps you full and satisfied for hours, which is perfect for those busy-bee days. The creamy sauce, olives, and fresh herbs elevate this recipe in true Mediterranean fashion, making it a satisfying breakfast or appetizing side dish.

## INGREDIENTS:

1½ cups vegetable stock

2 cups fresh cauliflower florets

4 hard-boiled eggs, peeled and cubed

¼ cup cherry tomatoes

2 tablespoons chopped fresh parsley

2 tablespoons chopped green onion

½ cup heavy cream

2 tablespoons light mayonnaise

1 tablespoon vinegar

1 teaspoon extra-virgin olive oil

4 black olives, sliced

## INSTRUCTIONS:

1. Pour the vegetable stock into an Instant Pot and insert the steamer basket.

2. Place the cauliflower florets in the steamer basket, seal the pot with the lid, and cook the cauliflower on high for 14 minutes.

3. Allow the pressure to release naturally for 4 minutes, then use the quick-release function and remove the lid.

4. Place the cauliflower florets in a large bowl. Add the hard-boiled eggs, cherry tomatoes, parsley, green onion, heavy cream, mayonnaise, vinegar, and olive oil, stirring to combine.

5. Garnish with black olives and divide among four serving bowls. Refrigerate leftovers in an airtight container for up to 3 days.

| NUTRITION · per one serving · % of Daily Value | | | | | |
|---|---|---|---|---|---|
| Calories | 180 | | Dietary Fiber | 3 g | 11% |
| Total Fat | 12 g | 15% | Total Sugars | 3 g | — |
| Saturated Fat | 5.1 g | 25% | Protein | 8 g | 16% |
| Polyunsaturated Fat | 1.6 g | — | Vitamin A | 805 mcg | 90% |
| Monounsaturated Fat | 4.2 g | — | Vitamin C | 30.3 mg | 35% |
| Trans Fat | — | — | Vitamin D | 1 mcg | 4% |
| Cholesterol | 185 mg | 62% | Potassium | 327 mg | 6% |
| Sodium | 105 mg | 5% | Calcium | 62 mg | 4% |
| Total Carbohydrates | 10 g | 4% | Iron | 1.5 mg | 8% |

# Breakfast Potato Salad

**Servings: 4**

**PREP TIME:** 10 minutes | **COOK TIME:** 15 minutes | **TOTAL TIME:** 25 minutes

Level 3: Moderate

Potatoes come in so many forms for breakfast recipes—hash browns, home fries, pancakes, and more. This dish takes a Mediterranean approach with steamed baby red potatoes, sweet balsamic vinegar, and sharp, pungent raw onions. Instead of overloading on sodium, you'll fill up on vitamin C, potassium, and fiber!

## INGREDIENTS:

1½ cups water

2 pounds baby red potatoes, peeled and quartered

¼ cup balsamic vinegar

¼ cup extra-virgin olive oil

1 small onion, chopped

2 teaspoons chopped parsley

1 teaspoon chopped thyme

1 teaspoon salt

½ teaspoon ground black pepper

## INSTRUCTIONS:

1. Place the water into an Instant Pot, then insert the steamer basket. Add the baby potatoes to the steamer basket.

2. Set the Instant Pot to non-venting, seal with the lid, and cook the potatoes on high for 12 minutes, until tender.

3. Switch to venting and allow the pressure to release naturally for 10 minutes, then switch to the quick-release function.

4. Remove the lid and place the potatoes into a large mixing bowl. Add the balsamic vinegar, olive oil, onion, parsley, thyme, salt, and pepper, tossing to combine. Divide among four serving bowls. Refrigerate leftovers in an airtight container for up to 3 days.

| NUTRITION · per one serving · % of Daily Value | | | | | |
|---|---|---|---|---|---|
| Calories | 230 | | Dietary Fiber | 4 g | 14% |
| Total Fat | 6 g | 8% | Total Sugars | 5 g | — |
| Saturated Fat | 0.8 g | 4% | Protein | 5 g | 10% |
| Polyunsaturated Fat | 0.7 g | — | Vitamin A | 23.4 mcg | 2% |
| Monounsaturated Fat | 3.9 g | — | Vitamin C | 22 mg | 25% |
| Trans Fat | — | — | Vitamin D | — | — |
| Cholesterol | — | — | Potassium | 1080 mg | 25% |
| Sodium | 45 mg | 2% | Calcium | 42 mg | 4% |
| Total Carbohydrates | 40 g | 15% | Iron | 1.9 mg | 10% |

**GF**
**SF**
**NF**
**VE**

# Mediterranean Frittata

**Servings: 2**

**PREP TIME:** 5 minutes I **COOK TIME:** 20 minutes I **TOTAL TIME:** 25 minutes

Level 3: Moderate

Swap out your regular omelets for this Mediterranean Frittata. Packed with briny feta, juicy cherry tomatoes, and fresh chives, it's perfectly seasoned and bakes in less than 15 minutes! Loaded with protein and linked to reduced heart disease and increased eye health, eggs are a reliable ingredient for your busy mornings.

## INGREDIENTS:

6 large eggs

¼ cup chopped chives

Handful of fresh basil

2 tablespoons heavy cream

1 teaspoon Italian seasoning

1 teaspoon Himalayan salt

½ teaspoon ground black pepper

½ cup crumbled feta cheese, divided

1 tablespoon extra-virgin olive oil

½ bell pepper, chopped

½ cup halved cherry tomatoes, divided

## INSTRUCTIONS:

1. Preheat the oven to 400°F.

2. Whisk the eggs, chives, basil, heavy cream, Italian seasoning, salt, and pepper together in a large bowl until well combined. Whisk in 6 tablespoons of the feta and set aside.

3. Heat the olive oil in a 9-inch oven-safe skillet over medium-high heat. Add the bell peppers and sauté for 4–5 minutes, until they soften. Stir in ¼ cup of the cherry tomatoes and cook for an additional 1–2 minutes, until tender.

4. Add the sautéed bell peppers and tomatoes to the egg mixture and stir with a spatula to distribute the vegetables, then add the remaining 2 tablespoons of feta and ¼ cup of cherry tomatoes. Mix to combine.

5. Pour the batter into the oven-safe skillet and return to medium-high heat for 1 minute, until the perimeter is slightly golden. Transfer the skillet to the oven and bake for 10–15 minutes, until the eggs are set.

6. Remove from the oven and transfer it to a wire rack to cool. Divide between two plates and serve!

| NUTRITION · per one serving · % of Daily Value | | | | | |
|---|---|---|---|---|---|
| Calories | 350 | | Dietary Fiber | 1 g | 3% |
| Total Fat | 25 g | 32% | Total Sugars | 3 g | — |
| Saturated Fat | 10.7 g | 54% | Protein | 25 g | 50% |
| Polyunsaturated Fat | 3.2 g | — | Vitamin A | 466 mcg | 50% |
| Monounsaturated Fat | 8.9 g | — | Vitamin C | 33.6 mg | 35% |
| Trans Fat | — | — | Vitamin D | 3.3 mcg | 15% |
| Cholesterol | 420 mg | 140% | Potassium | 395 mg | 8% |
| Sodium | 370 mg | 16% | Calcium | 292 mg | 20% |
| Total Carbohydrates | 6 g | 2% | Iron | 3.2 mg | 20% |

# Cinnamon Roll Porridge with Cranberries

**Servings: 1**

**PREP TIME:** 5 minutes | **TOTAL TIME:** 5 minutes | **TOTAL TIME:** 10 minutes

Level 2: Easy

Imagine biting into a fresh, crisp French pastry as part of your morning routine. Thanks to this recipe, you don't have to dream it up—you can experience all the flavors of a fruit-studded cinnamon roll in a quick, healthy oatmeal porridge! Rich cinnamon, syrupy honey, and tart cranberries come together to create a delicious and nutritious breakfast.

## INGREDIENTS:

1 cup non-dairy milk

½ cup gluten-free quick oats

1 banana, mashed, plus ¼ banana, sliced

1 teaspoon ground cardamom

1 teaspoon raw honey

¼ cup dried cranberries

1 teaspoon ground cinnamon

2 tablespoons almond butter

## INSTRUCTIONS:

1. Combine the milk, oats, mashed banana, cardamom, and honey in a small saucepan over medium-high heat. Cook for 5 minutes, stirring occasionally, until it thickens.

2. Transfer to a small heat-safe bowl, add the cranberries and cinnamon, and mix until well combined.

3. Top with the almond butter and banana slices. Serve immediately or refrigerate for the next day and serve cold.

| NUTRITION · per one serving · % of Daily Value | | | | | |
|---|---|---|---|---|---|
| Calories | 310 | | Dietary Fiber | 10 g | 36% |
| Total Fat | 11 g | 14% | Total Sugars | 12 g | — |
| Saturated Fat | 4.4 g | 22% | Protein | 15 g | 30% |
| Polyunsaturated Fat | 1.9 g | — | Vitamin A | 109 mcg | 10% |
| Monounsaturated Fat | 3.5 g | — | Vitamin C | 5 mg | 6% |
| *Trans* Fat | — | — | Vitamin D | 0.1 mcg | — |
| Cholesterol | 20 mg | 7% | Potassium | 701 mg | 15% |
| Sodium | 90 mg | 4% | Calcium | 296 mg | 25% |
| Total Carbohydrates | 56 g | 20% | Iron | — | — |

# Zucchini, Pea, & Halloumi Fritters

**Makes 10 pancakes**

**PREP TIME:** 10 minutes I **COOK TIME:** 15 minutes I **TOTAL TIME:** 25 minutes

Level 3: Moderate

Traditionally made from a mixture of sheep and goat milk, Halloumi dates back to 1191! Loaded with protein and calcium, this salty cheese elevates any recipe—including these fritters. Thanks to the zucchini, this dish may improve digestion, strengthen eyesight, and aid weight loss!

## INGREDIENTS:

3 medium zucchinis, grated

1 cup coarsely grated Halloumi

1 cup almond flour

½ cup frozen peas

¼ cup chopped fresh dill or mint

2 eggs, lightly beaten

1½ teaspoons Himalayan salt

½ teaspoon ground black pepper

3 tablespoons extra-virgin olive oil

## INSTRUCTIONS:

1. Combine the zucchini, Halloumi, almond flour, peas, dill or mint, eggs, salt, and black pepper in a medium bowl and mix well.

2. Place the olive oil in a large frying pan over medium-high heat.

3. Spoon about 3 tablespoons of the batter per pancake into the frying pan and flatten slightly using a spatula.

4. Cook the pancakes for 3–4 minutes each, flipping halfway through, until golden. Place them onto paper towels to drain.

5. Repeat steps 3–4 until all the batter has been used.

6. Serve warm. Refrigerate leftovers in an airtight container for up to 3 days.

| NUTRITION · per one serving · % of Daily Value | | | | | |
|---|---|---|---|---|---|
| Calories | 60 | | Dietary Fiber | – | – |
| Total Fat | 4.5 g | 6% | Total Sugars | – | – |
| Saturated Fat | 1.8 g | 9% | Protein | 4 g | 8% |
| Polyunsaturated Fat | 0.3 g | – | Vitamin A | 47.7 mcg | 6% |
| Monounsaturated Fat | 1.7 g | – | Vitamin C | 2.5 mg | 2% |
| Trans Fat | – | – | Vitamin D | 0.2 mcg | – |
| Cholesterol | 15 mg | 5% | Potassium | 50 mg | 2% |
| Sodium | 85 mg | 4% | Calcium | 92 mg | 8% |
| Total Carbohydrates | 2 g | 1% | Iron | 0.4 mg | 2% |

SF
NF
EF
DF

# Golden Shrimp & Avocado Toast

**Servings: 4**

**PREP TIME:** 25 minutes | **COOK TIME:** 5 minutes | **TOTAL TIME:** 30 minutes

Level 3: Moderate

Seafood has been fundamental to Mediterranean cuisine since its creation. This recipe encompasses a fan favorite—juicy shrimp. Toss it with lime juice and paprika and layered it with fresh avocado slices, and you'll wonder why you didn't experiment with shrimp for breakfast *before*!

## INGREDIENTS:

1 pound shrimp, raw

Juice of 2 limes, divided

1 teaspoon smoked paprika

½ teaspoon kosher salt

¼ teaspoon cayenne pepper

4 slices whole-wheat bread, toasted

4 large avocados, sliced

½ large tomato, chopped

¼ cup chopped fresh cilantro, optional

## INSTRUCTIONS:

1. Combine the shrimp, juice of 1 lime, smoked paprika, salt, and cayenne pepper in a medium bowl, tossing to combine. Cover the bowl with a dishtowel or plastic wrap and refrigerate for 15–20 minutes to marinate.

2. Turn your grill to high. Arrange the shrimp on the grill and cook for 3–4 minutes, until golden.

3. Place the toast slices on a platter, then arrange the avocado slices on the toast. Top with the shrimp and garnish with the remaining lime juice, the tomatoes, and cilantro, if desired. Serve warm.

| NUTRITION · per one serving · % of Daily Value | | | | | |
|---|---|---|---|---|---|
| Calories | 470 | | Dietary Fiber | 15 g | 54% |
| Total Fat | 30 g | 38% | Total Sugars | 2 g | — |
| Saturated Fat | 4.4 g | 22% | Protein | 29 g | 58% |
| Polyunsaturated Fat | 4 g | — | Vitamin A | 273 mcg | 30% |
| Monounsaturated Fat | 19.8 g | — | Vitamin C | 31.1 mg | 35% |
| *Trans* Fat | — | — | Vitamin D | — | — |
| Cholesterol | 135 mg | 45% | Potassium | 1406 mg | 30% |
| Sodium | 115 mg | 5% | Calcium | 108 mg | 8% |
| Total Carbohydrates | 28 g | 10% | Iron | 2.4 mg | 15% |

**SF**
**GF**
**VE**
**NF**
**DF**

# Spinach Fritters

**Servings: 6**

**PREP TIME:** 5 minutes I **COOK TIME:** 25 minutes I **TOTAL TIME:** 30 minutes

Level 4: Challenging

As a Recipe and Lifestyle Coach, fiber is one of my favorite things, since it can aid weight loss, keep you satisfied, and *control* your blood sugar levels! Thankfully, both potatoes and spinach are treasure-troves of fiber. If you have any leftover veggies lying around, this recipe is the perfect way to put them to use.

## INGREDIENTS:

1 tablespoon
+ 2 teaspoons
extra-virgin olive oil,
divided

1 cup diced potatoes

1 medium onion, diced

1 garlic clove, minced

½ cup spinach leaves

1⅓ cups chickpea flour

2 large eggs, lightly
beaten

½ cup water

½ teaspoon salt

## INSTRUCTIONS:

1. Heat 1 tablespoon of olive oil in a non-stick frying pan over medium-high heat. Stir in the diced potatoes and cook for 10 minutes, until they are lightly golden and start to soften.

2. Add the onion, garlic, and remaining 2 teaspoons of olive oil. Cook for another 5 minutes, stirring occasionally, until the onions soften.

3. Add the spinach and cook for 2 minutes, until the spinach wilts.

4. Whisk together the chickpea flour, eggs, water, and salt in a medium bowl. Pour the mixture into the pan and mix well, until the potatoes are coated with the mixture.

5. Decrease the heat to medium-low and cook for 5–7 minutes, until golden. Flip and cook for another 5 minutes, until golden. Remove from the heat.

6. Serve and enjoy! Refrigerate leftovers in an airtight container for up to 3 days.

**NUTRITION** · per one serving · % of Daily Value

| | | | | | |
|---|---|---|---|---|---|
| Calories | 45 | | Dietary Fiber | 1 g | 4% |
| Total Fat | 1.5 g | 2% | Total Sugars | 1 g | — |
| Saturated Fat | 0.2 g | 1% | Protein | 1 g | 2% |
| Polyunsaturated Fat | 0.1 g | — | Vitamin A | 141 mcg | 15% |
| Monounsaturated Fat | 1.1 g | — | Vitamin C | 7.8 mg | 8% |
| *Trans* Fat | — | — | Vitamin D | — | — |
| Cholesterol | — | — | Potassium | 165 mg | 4% |
| Sodium | 5 mg | — | Calcium | 17 mg | 2% |
| Total Carbohydrates | 7 g | 3% | Iron | 0.5 mg | 2% |

# Pesto & Avocado
# Poached Eggs on Toast

**Servings: 2**

**PREP TIME:** 10 minutes | **COOK TIME:** 10 minutes | **TOTAL TIME:** 25 minutes

Level 3: Moderate

Avocado toast has been a winning combination for years! Uplifted by fresh pesto, peppery parsley, and savory eggs, this recipe is part of our weekly repertoire in my home. If you're new to poaching eggs, the secret is to keep the water swirling the entire time.

## INGREDIENTS:

2 slices whole-wheat bread, toasted

¼ cup pesto

1 avocado, sliced

2 tablespoons white vinegar

1 ¼ teaspoons salt, divided

2 medium eggs

½ medium red pepper, finely diced

¼ teaspoon ground black pepper

10 parsley leaves, finely chopped

## INSTRUCTIONS:

1. Arrange the toast slices on a platter and spread a generous amount of pesto over each slice.

2. Place the avocado slices on top of the pesto.

3. Fill a large saucepan with water and bring to a boil over medium-high heat.

4. Reduce the heat to low and keep the water at a gentle boil. Add the white vinegar and 1 teaspoon of salt and stir the water in a circular motion to create a vortex at the center of the pot. Carefully crack one egg into the center and keep stirring to maintain the water's vortex while the egg cooks. Adjust the heat, if needed, to maintain the gentle boil. Cook for 3½ minutes, until the egg white is firm and the yolk is loose.

5. Carefully scoop the poached egg out of the water and place it on top of one slice of avocado toast.

6. Repeat steps 4–5 for the remaining egg.

7. Top the poached eggs with diced red pepper and sprinkle them with black pepper, the remaining ¼ teaspoon of salt, and parsley. Serve warm and enjoy!

**NUTRITION** · per one serving · % of Daily Value

| | | | | | |
|---|---|---|---|---|---|
| Calories | 582 | | Dietary Fiber | 11.4 g | 39% |
| Total Fat | 34.1 g | 44% | Total Sugars | 5.1 g | – |
| Saturated Fat | 6.4 g | 32% | Protein | 16.2 g | 32% |
| Polyunsaturated Fat | 5.1 g | – | Vitamin A | 979 mcg | 110% |
| Monounsaturated Fat | 19.5 g | – | Vitamin C | 75.6 mcg | 80% |
| Trans Fat | – | – | Vitamin D | 0.9 mcg | 4% |
| Cholesterol | 128 mg | 43% | Potassium | 875 mg | 20% |
| Sodium | 985 mg | 43% | Calcium | 169 mg | 15% |
| Total Carbohydrates | 31.4 g | 11% | Iron | 4.2 mg | 25% |

# Simple Cheese & Veggie Omelet

**Servings: 2**

**PREP TIME:** 5 minutes | **COOK TIME:** 5 minutes | **TOTAL TIME:** 10 minutes

Level 3: Moderate

If you're a gardener, try swapping in some of your fresh harvests for the fillings suggested here. And if you use locally sourced eggs, you'll dramatically reduce your meal's carbon footprint—in true Mediterranean fashion! What makes this omelet unique is the dynamic seasonings, including allspice, mint, and Spanish paprika.

## INGREDIENTS:

4 large eggs

2 tablespoons almond milk

1 teaspoon Himalayan salt

½ teaspoon ground black pepper

½ teaspoon Spanish paprika

¼ teaspoon ground allspice

¼ teaspoon baking powder

1½ teaspoons extra-virgin olive oil

3 tablespoons chopped fresh parsley

3 tablespoons chopped fresh mint

**Optional fillings:**

½ cup halved cherry tomatoes

2 tablespoons sliced and pitted Kalamata olives

¼–⅓ cup drained and quartered marinated artichoke hearts

2–4 tablespoons crumbled feta cheese, as desired

## INSTRUCTIONS:

1. Whisk together the eggs, almond milk, salt, pepper, paprika, allspice, and baking powder in medium bowl.

2. Heat the olive oil in a 10-inch skillet over medium-high heat. Tilt the skillet so the oil fully coats the bottom.

3. Pour the egg mixture into the skillet and stir it quickly with a spatula for 5 seconds. Push the cooked bits of the egg toward the center of the pan while tilting the pan to allow the raw egg to fill the empty spaces.

4. Cook the omelet for 1–2 minutes, until the bottom is golden and the eggs are nearly set, then remove from the heat. Add the toppings of your choice to one side of the omelet and fold over the empty side onto the toppings.

5. Slice the omelet in half, place each half on a serving plate, and sprinkle with parsley and mint, if desired.

**NUTRITION** · per one serving · % of Daily Value

| | | | | | |
|---|---|---|---|---|---|
| Calories | 180 | | Dietary Fiber | 2 g | 7% |
| Total Fat | 10 g | 13% | Total Sugars | 2 g | — |
| Saturated Fat | 3.2 g | 16% | Protein | 15 g | 30% |
| Polyunsaturated Fat | 2.1 g | — | Vitamin A | 690 mcg | 80% |
| Monounsaturated Fat | 3.4 g | — | Vitamin C | 70.8 mg | 80% |
| Trans Fat | — | — | Vitamin D | 2.2 mcg | 10% |
| Cholesterol | 170 mg | 57% | Potassium | 393 mg | 8% |
| Sodium | 125 mg | 5% | Calcium | 140 mg | 10% |
| Total Carbohydrates | 8 g | 3% | Iron | 2.9 mg | 15% |

# LUNCH

# Tuna Salad on Toast

**Servings: 4**

**PREP TIME:** 10 minutes I **COOK TIME:** 0 minutes | **TOTAL TIME:** 10 minutes

Level 1: Very Easy

Portofino tuna can be the focal point of any Mediterranean dish! Available in albacore or yellowfin cans, the fish adds a touch of elegance to this lunchtime classic. When you're low on time and need a quick snack, this vitamin $B_{12}$-packed recipe will always hit the spot.

## INGREDIENTS:

2 (5-oz.) cans tuna in water, drained

¼ cup light mayonnaise

1 stalk of celery, diced

2 tablespoons diced red onion

1–2 tablespoons chopped parsley, chives, or other herbs

½ tablespoon Dijon mustard

1 teaspoon ground black pepper

½ teaspoon salt

4 slices whole-wheat bread, toasted

## INSTRUCTIONS:

1. Combine the tuna, mayonnaise, celery, red onion, parsley, mustard, pepper, and salt in a bowl. Stir until thoroughly combined.

2. Spread the tuna salad over the toast slices and serve!

| NUTRITION · per one serving · % of Daily Value | | | | | |
|---|---|---|---|---|---|
| Calories | 254.62kcal | | Dietary Fiber | 3.14 g | 11% |
| Total Fat | 8.65 g | 12% | Total Sugars | 4.32 g | 5% |
| Saturated Fat | 1.3 g | 5% | Protein | 16 g | 30% |
| Polyunsaturated Fat | 1.3 g | — | Vitamin A | 212 mcg | 25% |
| Monounsaturated Fat | 3.3 g | — | Vitamin C | 33.6 mcg | 35% |
| Trans Fat | — | — | Vitamin D | 0.6 mcg | 4% |
| Cholesterol | 21.02 mg | 7% | Potassium | 209.1 mg | 6% |
| Sodium | 868.2 mg | 43% | Calcium | 53.98 mg | 7% |
| Total Carbohydrates | 28.19 g | 11% | Iron | 1.72 mg | 12% |

SF
EF
NF

# Chicken & Vegetable Wraps

**Servings: 4**

**PREP TIME:** 10 minutes | **COOK TIME:** 0 minutes | **TOTAL TIME:** 10 minutes

Level 1: Very Easy

The secret behind any great wrap is an irresistible combination of textures. Here, tender shredded chicken is paired with juicy cucumbers, crunchy carrots, and creamy yogurt. If you're prone to a growling tummy in the afternoon, try this protein-rich and vitamin-packed dish to keep you satisfied for hours!

## INGREDIENTS:

2 cups cooked chicken, shredded

½ cup diced English cucumber

½ cup chopped carrots

½ red bell pepper, diced

1 green onion, chopped

¼ cup plain Greek yogurt

1 tablespoon fresh lemon juice

½ teaspoon chopped fresh thyme

¼ teaspoon salt

¼ teaspoon ground black pepper

4 (8-inch) whole-wheat tortillas

## INSTRUCTIONS:

1. Combine the chicken, cucumber, carrots, red bell pepper, green onion, yogurt, lemon juice, thyme, salt, and pepper in a medium bowl and mix until combined.

2. Arrange the tortillas on separate serving plates and add one-quarter of the chicken salad to each tortilla.

3. Fold the tortillas around the chicken filling to create a pocket. Serve and enjoy! Refrigerate leftover chicken salad in an airtight container for up to 3 days.

| NUTRITION · per one serving · % of Daily Value | | | | | |
|---|---|---|---|---|---|
| Calories | 400 | | Dietary Fiber | 5 g | 18% |
| Total Fat | 26 g | 33% | Total Sugars | 2 g | — |
| Saturated Fat | 8.4 g | 42% | Protein | 17 g | 34% |
| Polyunsaturated Fat | 5.2 g | — | Vitamin A | 772 mcg | 90% |
| Monounsaturated Fat | 10.8 g | — | Vitamin C | 17.6 mg | 20% |
| *Trans* Fat | — | — | Vitamin D | 0.1 Mcg | — |
| Cholesterol | 35 mg | 12% | Potassium | 314 mg | 6% |
| Sodium | 210 mg | 9% | Calcium | 134 mg | 10% |
| Total Carbohydrates | 22 g | 8% | Iron | 2.1 mg | 10% |

# Berry & Burrata Summer Salad

**Servings: 4**

**PREP TIME:** 10 minutes | **COOK TIME:** 0 minutes | **TOTAL TIME:** 10 minutes

Level 1: Very Easy

This spunky salad is a twist on the classic Caprese. Swap out tomatoes for berries, pair with seasonal greens and fresh lemon juice, and you've got summer in a bowl! Fiber- and antioxidant-rich, this recipe will have your al fresco-dining guests singing your praises.

## INGREDIENTS:

3 tablespoons extra-virgin olive oil

Juice of 1 large lemon

½ teaspoon kosher salt

½ teaspoon ground black pepper

6 ounces baby arugula

6 ounces fresh blackberries

6 ounces fresh raspberries

6 ounces fresh strawberries

1 small shallot, halved and sliced

4 ounces burrata cheese, sliced

## INSTRUCTIONS:

1. To make the dressing, whisk together the extra-virgin olive oil, lemon juice, salt, and pepper in a small bowl until combined.

2. Combine the arugula, blackberries, raspberries, strawberries, and shallot in a large bowl. Pour the dressing over and toss to combine.

3. Divide the salad among four serving plates and top with the burrata. Serve and enjoy!

| NUTRITION · per one serving · % of Daily Value | | | | | |
|---|---|---|---|---|---|
| Calories | 240 | | Dietary Fiber | 7 g | 25% |
| Total Fat | 17 g | 22% | Total Sugars | 5 g | — |
| Saturated Fat | 5.2 g | 26% | Protein | 7 g | 14% |
| Polyunsaturated Fat | 1.7 g | — | Vitamin A | 431 mcg | 50% |
| Monounsaturated Fat | 9.2 g | — | Vitamin C | 83.4 mg | 90% |
| Trans Fat | — | — | Vitamin D | 0.2 mcg | — |
| Cholesterol | 15 mg | 5% | Potassium | 475 mg | 10% |
| Sodium | 280 mg | 12% | Calcium | 260 mg | 20% |
| Total Carbohydrates | 18 g | 7% | Iron | 1.6 mg | 8% |

GF
NF
VE
EF
DF

# Orange & Pomegranate Salad

**Servings: 6**

**PREP TIME:** 15 minutes | **COOK TIME:** 0 minutes | **TOTAL TIME:** 15 minutes

Level 2: Easy

Who said salads are only for vegetables? Bright oranges and pomegranate seeds are the base of this lively salad with a Mediterranean twist. Picture yourself in your backyard, facing the sun, while enjoying this refreshing salad. Unquestionably, this meal will lift your mood!

## INGREDIENTS:

1 tablespoon extra-virgin olive oil

1 tablespoon honey

Juice of 1 lime

1½ teaspoons orange blossom water, optional

1 cup thinly sliced red onions

25 fresh mint leaves, chopped

6 navel oranges, peeled and sliced into rounds

⅛ teaspoon kosher salt

⅛ teaspoon sweet paprika

⅛ teaspoon ground cinnamon

Seeds (arils) of 1 pomegranate

## INSTRUCTIONS:

1. Whisk together the olive oil, honey, lime juice, and orange blossom water, if using, in a small bowl and set aside.

2. Place the red onions into a small bowl of ice water and set aside for 5 minutes to allow their flavor to mellow. Drain the onions and dry thoroughly.

3. Arrange half of the mint leaves around the edge of a serving bowl.

4. Place the orange slices and onions in the bowl and sprinkle with the salt, paprika, and cinnamon.

5. Drizzle the dressing over the salad, add the pomegranate seeds and remaining mint leaves, and set aside for 5 minutes to allow the flavors to blend. Serve and enjoy!

| NUTRITION · per one serving · % of Daily Value | | | | | |
|---|---|---|---|---|---|
| Calories | 140 | | Dietary Fiber | 8 g | 21% |
| Total Fat | 3 g | 4% | Total Sugars | 12 g | — |
| Saturated Fat | 0.4 g | 2% | Protein | 2 g | 4% |
| Polyunsaturated Fat | 0.3 g | — | Vitamin A | 124 mcg | 15% |
| Monounsaturated Fat | 1.7 g | — | Vitamin C | 71.5 mg | 80% |
| Trans Fat | — | — | Vitamin D | — | — |
| Cholesterol | — | — | Potassium | 376 mg | 8% |
| Sodium | — | — | Calcium | 71 mg | 6% |
| Total Carbohydrates | 29 g | 11% | Iron | 0.4 mg | 2% |

# Watermelon & Feta Salad

**Servings: 6**

**PREP TIME:** 15 minutes | **COOK TIME:** 0 minutes | **TOTAL TIME:** 15 minutes

Level 2: Easy

If you love salty and sweet duos, this salad is for you! Once summer rolls around, I love to experiment with seasonal produce. I recently spotted a ginormous watermelon at my local farmer's market and knew it was destined for feta—a match made in Mediterranean heaven.

## INGREDIENTS:

2 tablespoons honey

2 tablespoons lime juice

1–2 tablespoons extra-virgin olive oil

¼ teaspoon salt

½ watermelon, peeled and cubed

1 English cucumber, cubed (about 2 cups)

15 fresh mint leaves, chopped

15 fresh basil leaves, chopped

½ cup crumbled feta cheese

## INSTRUCTIONS:

1. Whisk the honey, lime juice, olive oil, and salt together in a small bowl and set aside.

2. Combine the watermelon, cucumber, mint, and basil in a serving bowl, mixing well.

3. Drizzle the dressing over the salad, tossing carefully to combine. Top with the feta and serve. Refrigerate leftovers in an airtight container for up to 3 days.

| NUTRITION · per one serving · % of Daily Value | | | | | |
|---|---|---|---|---|---|
| Calories | 130 | | Dietary Fiber | 1 g | 4% |
| Total Fat | 5 g | 6% | Total Sugars | 11 g | — |
| Saturated Fat | 2.2 g | 11% | Protein | 4 g | 8% |
| Polyunsaturated Fat | 0.4 g | — | Vitamin A | 330 mcg | 35% |
| Monounsaturated Fat | 2.2 g | — | Vitamin C | 16.4 mcg | 20% |
| Trans Fat | — | — | Vitamin D | 0.05 mcg | — |
| Cholesterol | 10 mg | 3% | Potassium | 254 mg | 6% |
| Sodium | 90 mg | 4% | Calcium | 82 mg | 6% |
| Total Carbohydrates | 20 g | 7% | Iron | 0.6 mg | 4% |

# Prosciutto Salad

GF
SF
EF
NF
DF

**Servings: 4**

**PREP TIME:** 10 minutes | **COOK TIME:** 0 minutes | **TOTAL TIME:** 10 minutes

Level 2: Easy

Italians are known for their pizzas and pastas, but their prosciutto is a secret weapon. Traditionally paired with melon as an appetizer, prosciutto is a salty dry-cured ham that boasts plenty of protein and healthy fats. Here it takes the spotlight in a salad, cast with peppery arugula and juicy tomatoes.

## INGREDIENTS:

7 ounces prosciutto, roughly chopped

2 cucumbers, diced

2 cups arugula, torn

1 cup halved cherry tomatoes

2 tablespoons extra-virgin olive oil

1 tablespoon mustard

1 tablespoon lemon juice

¼ teaspoon dried oregano

¼ teaspoon dried dill

¼ teaspoon dried basil

## INSTRUCTIONS:

1. Combine the prosciutto, cucumbers, arugula, and cherry tomatoes in a medium bowl, tossing well.

2. Whisk the olive oil, mustard, lemon juice, oregano, dill, and basil together in a small bowl.

3. Pour the dressing over the prosciutto salad and toss to combine. Serve and enjoy!

| NUTRITION · per one serving · % of Daily Value | | | | | |
|---|---|---|---|---|---|
| Calories | 130 | | Dietary Fiber | 1 g | 4% |
| Total Fat | 9 g | 12% | Total Sugars | 1 g | — |
| Saturated Fat | 0.8 g | 4% | Protein | 10 g | 20% |
| Polyunsaturated Fat | 2.2 g | — | Vitamin A | 0.35 mcg | 0% |
| Monounsaturated Fat | 5.4 g | — | Vitamin C | 6.4 mg | 8% |
| Trans Fat | — | — | Vitamin D | 0.05 mcg | — |
| Cholesterol | 20 mg | 7% | Potassium | 435 mg | 10% |
| Sodium | 280 mg | 17% | Calcium | 40 mg | 4% |
| Total Carbohydrates | 4 g | 1% | Iron | 0.8 mg | 4% |

**GF**
**VE**
**EF**
**NF**

# Caprese Salad

**Servings: 4**

**PREP TIME:** 10 minutes | **COOK TIME:** 0 minutes | **TOTAL TIME:** 10 minutes

Level 2: Easy

Sometimes nothing quite hits the spot like a traditional Caprese Salad. The flavor of this recipe depends entirely on your choice of tomatoes. For a classic Caprese, go for full-flavored Romas. If you're in the mood for something sweet, try Cocktail tomatoes. And if you prefer tangy, opt for an heirloom variety!

## INGREDIENTS:

3 large tomatoes, sliced

8 ounces mozzarella, sliced

¼ cup fresh basil leaves

2 tablespoons extra-virgin olive oil

1 tablespoon balsamic reduction or balsamic glaze

½ teaspoon salt

½ teaspoon ground black pepper

## INSTRUCTIONS:

1. Place a slice of tomato on a serving platter, then layer a slice of mozzarella cheese on top, just slightly to the side. Alternate layers of tomato and mozzarella slices until both ingredients are gone and you've formed a spiral.

2. Arrange the fresh basil leaves between the tomato and cheese slices.

3. Pour the olive oil and balsamic reduction over the Caprese salad, then sprinkle the salt and pepper on top. Serve immediately.

| NUTRITION · per one serving · % of Daily Value | | | | | |
|---|---|---|---|---|---|
| Calories | 140 | | Dietary Fiber | 1 g | 4% |
| Total Fat | 7 g | 9% | Total Sugars | 1 g | – |
| Saturated Fat | 0.9 g | 5% | Protein | 18 g | 36% |
| Polyunsaturated Fat | 0.7 g | – | Vitamin A | 112 mcg | 10% |
| Monounsaturated Fat | 4.9 g | – | Vitamin C | 1.6 mcg | 2% |
| Trans Fat | – | – | Vitamin D | – | – |
| Cholesterol | 10 mg | 3% | Potassium | 92 mg | 2% |
| Sodium | 210 mg | 9% | Calcium | 547 mg | 40% |
| Total Carbohydrates | 3 g | 1% | Iron | 0.3 mg | 2% |

# Avocado Seafood Wraps

**Servings: 3**

**PREP TIME:** 10 minutes | **COOK TIME:** 5 minutes | **TOTAL TIME:** 15 minutes

Level 3: Moderate

You won't believe that these wraps come together in just fifteen minutes. Perfect for prepared-in-advance work lunches or for an al fresco summer appetizer, they feature tender shrimp, meaty crab, and creamy avocado, all perfectly spiced and swaddled in a warm tortilla.

## INGREDIENTS:

5 ounces shrimp, peeled and deveined

3 ounces crab meat, finely chopped

¼ cup heavy cream

1 teaspoon unsalted butter

¾ teaspoon ground coriander

½ teaspoon ground cayenne pepper

¼ teaspoon minced garlic

2 tablespoons plain Greek yogurt

3 (8-inch) whole-wheat tortillas

1 avocado, sliced

1 cucumber, sliced

2 tablespoons parsley, optional

## INSTRUCTIONS:

1. Combine the shrimp, crab meat, heavy cream, butter, garlic, coriander, and cayenne pepper in a large saucepan over medium-high heat. Cook for 5–6 minutes, stirring occasionally, until the shrimp is bright pink. Remove from the heat and set aside.

2. Spread the yogurt onto the tortillas.

3. Arrange the avocado and cucumber on the tortillas, then add the seafood mixture.

4. Roll the tortillas up over the filling, folding in the sides, and use a toothpick to prevent the filling from falling out. Serve immediately.

| NUTRITION · per one serving · % of Daily Value | | | | | |
|---|---|---|---|---|---|
| Calories | 337 | | Dietary Fiber | 7.22 g | 26% |
| Total Fat | 18 g | 27% | Total Sugars | 3.27 g | — |
| Saturated Fat | 8.53 g | 43% | Protein | 18 g | 36% |
| Polyunsaturated Fat | 1.9 g | — | Vitamin A | 170 mcg | 20% |
| Monounsaturated Fat | 8.2 g | — | Vitamin C | 11.8 mg | 15% |
| Trans Fat | 0.25 g | — | Vitamin D | 0.1 mcg | — |
| Cholesterol | 90 mg | 30% | Potassium | 718 mg | 15% |
| Sodium | 720 mg | 36% | Calcium | 180.88 mg | 23% |
| Total Carbohydrates | 25.21 g | 10% | Iron | 1.96 mg | 14% |

SF
NF
VE
DF

# Savory Mushroom & Leek Galette

**Servings: 8**

**PREP TIME:** 5 minutes | **COOK TIME:** 30 minutes | **TOTAL TIME:** 35 minutes

Level 4: Challenging

When it comes to vegetarian dishes, mushrooms reign as champion! They give this savory galette a meaty, earthy flavor, while upping your protein, fiber, and vitamin intake. Paired with fresh leek and a buttery dough, they make this recipe one you'll have bookmarked for years to come.

## INGREDIENTS:

¼ cup extra-virgin olive oil, divided

1 large leek (white parts only), finely chopped

1 tablespoon kosher salt

½ tablespoon ground black pepper

½ teaspoon ground red pepper flakes

1 pound mushrooms, sliced

⅓ cup frozen peas

3 fresh thyme sprigs, leaves only

1 rolled store-bought pie crust or 1 batch homemade pie dough

1 tablespoon nutritional yeast

1 large egg, beaten

1 teaspoon flaky sea salt

## INSTRUCTIONS:

1. Preheat the oven to 425°F.

2. Heat 3 tablespoons of the olive oil in a large skillet over medium-high heat.

3. Add the leeks, kosher salt, pepper, and red pepper flakes and cook, stirring periodically, for 4 minutes, until the leeks soften.

4. Push the leeks to one side of the pan, then add the mushrooms and the remaining 1 tablespoon of olive oil.

5. Cook for 10 minutes, until the mushrooms' juices evaporate, then mix in the peas and thyme and cook for 1 minute, until the peas thaw. Remove from the heat.

6. Meanwhile, place a large piece of parchment paper down on a flat countertop. Roll the dough out on the parchment into a 9-inch circle about ¼ inch thick.

7. Transfer the parchment with the dough to a large baking sheet.

*recipe continues*

8. Sprinkle the nutritional yeast on top of the dough and press it in using your fingers.

9. Pour the mushroom-leek mixture over the middle of the dough, then spread the filling into an even layer, leaving a 1-inch border around the edges of the dough.

10. Fold the edges of the pie dough over the mushroom-leek mixture, overlapping them to seal the edges.

11. Brush the dough with the egg and sprinkle with the sea salt.

12. Bake the mushroom–leek galette for 20–25 minutes, until golden.

13. Remove from the oven and allow to cool on the pan for 5 minutes. Cut the galette into eight even portions and serve. Refrigerate leftovers in an airtight container for up to 3 days.

**NUTRITION** · per one serving · % of Daily Value

| | | | | | |
|---|---|---|---|---|---|
| Calories | 220 | | Dietary Fiber | 2 g | 7% |
| Total Fat | 15 g | 19% | Total Sugars | 2 g | — |
| Saturated Fat | 3.9 g | 20% | Protein | 4 g | 8% |
| Polyunsaturated Fat | 1.8 g | — | Vitamin A | 113 mcg | 15% |
| Monounsaturated Fat | 8.1 g | — | Vitamin C | 20.4 mg | 25% |
| Trans Fat | — | — | Vitamin D | 0.3 mcg | 2% |
| Cholesterol | 25 mg | 8% | Potassium | 312 mg | 6% |
| Sodium | 190 mg | 8% | Calcium | 27 mg | 2% |
| Total Carbohydrates | 20 g | 7% | Iron | 1.4 mg | 8% |

# Shrimp Crêpes

**Makes 4 crêpes**

**PREP TIME:** 5 minutes | **COOK TIME:** 10 minutes | **TOTAL TIME:** 15 minutes

Level 3: Moderate

Crêpes don't always have to be sweet! Instead of topping them with a dollop of whipped cream and a drizzle of syrup, this version balances savory shrimp with creamy mozzarella. The secret to turning out perfect crêpes is to use a rubber spatula to loosen the edge of the crêpe once it releases from the pan, then use your fingers to gently flip.

## INGREDIENTS:

1 cup 2% milk

1 large egg, beaten

1½ tablespoons unsalted butter, melted, plus more for the pan

1 cup flour

1 tablespoon granulated sugar

2 teaspoons salt, divided

2 teaspoons dried oregano, divided

1 teaspoon extra-virgin olive oil

1 cup peeled, deveined, and boiled shrimp

⅓ cup shredded mozzarella cheese

## INSTRUCTIONS:

1. Whisk the milk, egg, butter, flour, sugar, 1 teaspoon salt, and 1 teaspoon oregano together in a large bowl.

2. Heat about ½ tablespoon of butter in a small skillet over medium to high heat.

3. Ladle ¼ cup of the batter into the skillet and swirl it around until it coats the entire bottom. If the batter is not evenly distributed, you can spread it out with a spatula. Cook for 30 seconds, then gently flip the crêpe. Cook for 30 more seconds, then remove from the pan and set aside.

4. Repeat step 3 with the rest of the batter. You may need to add more butter to the skillet between each crêpe.

*recipe continues*

5. Heat the olive oil in a separate skillet over medium-high heat. Once shimmering, add the shrimp, mozzarella, and remaining 1 teaspoon each oregano and salt. Cook, stirring occasionally, for 5 minutes, until the shrimp is bright pink. Remove the skillet from the heat.

6. Place ⅓ cup of the shrimp filling on each crêpe and roll to enclose the filling.

7. Top your crêpes with any leftover filling, if desired, and serve!

| NUTRITION · per one serving · % of Daily Value | | | | | |
|---|---|---|---|---|---|
| Calories | 288 | | Dietary Fiber | 1.15 g | 4% |
| Total Fat | 12.22 g | 17% | Total Sugars | 6.25 g | – |
| Saturated Fat | 6.39 g | 32% | Protein | 14 g | 27% |
| Polyunsaturated Fat | 0.85 g | – | Vitamin A | 25.5 mcg | 2% |
| Monounsaturated Fat | 3.92 g | – | Vitamin C | – | – |
| Trans Fat | 0.01 g | – | Vitamin D | 0.025 mcg | – |
| Cholesterol | 80.32 mg | 27% | Potassium | 242.18 mg | 7% |
| Sodium | 850.73 mg | 43% | Calcium | 163.23 mg | 20% |
| Total Carbohydrates | 30.39 g | 12% | Iron | 0.96 mg | 7% |

# Mediterranean Quiche

**Servings: 6**

**PREP TIME:** 10 minutes | **COOK TIME:** 25 minutes | **TOTAL TIME:** 35 minutes

Level 3: Moderate

Pop a bite of this quiche in your mouth for instant satisfaction! Most—if not all—of these ingredients are already in your kitchen, which makes this lunch a great way to use up what you already have. The key ingredient is the cream cheese, which enhances the velvety texture of the filling.

## INGREDIENTS:

1 cup whole-wheat flour

½ teaspoon salt

⅓ cup unsalted butter, softened

4 eggs, beaten

1 cup shredded mozzarella cheese

3 tablespoons chopped chives

1 tablespoon cream cheese

1 teaspoon dried oregano

½ teaspoon ground paprika

## INSTRUCTIONS:

1. Preheat the oven to 365°F.

2. Whisk together the flour and salt in the bowl of a stand mixer fitted with the dough attachment, then add the butter and mix until the dough pulls away from the sides of the bowl without leaving much of a sticky residue.

3. Roll out the dough between two sheets of parchment until it is 9 inches round and about ¼ inch thick. Remove the top piece of parchment. Transfer the dough with the bottom parchment paper to a 9-inch round pie pan and gently press the dough into the pan. Bake for 10 minutes, until golden.

4. While baking, whisk the eggs, mozzarella, chives, cream cheese, oregano, and paprika together in a medium bowl.

5. Remove the crust from the oven and place it into the refrigerator for 5 minutes.

6. Pour the egg–cheese mixture into the crust, spreading it into an even layer, and bake for 10 minutes, until golden. Remove from the oven and allow to cool for 5 minutes.

7. Slice and serve immediately, or chill the quiche for 4–6 hours before serving. Refrigerate leftovers in an airtight container for up to three days.

| NUTRITION · per one serving · % of Daily Value | | | | | |
|---|---|---|---|---|---|
| Calories | 220 | | Dietary Fiber | 1 g | 4% |
| Total Fat | 10 g | 13% | Total Sugars | 1 g | — |
| Saturated Fat | 5.6 g | 28% | Protein | 12 g | 24% |
| Polyunsaturated Fat | 0.9 g | — | Vitamin A | 195 mcg | 20% |
| Monounsaturated Fat | 3.2 g | — | Vitamin C | 0.9 mg | — |
| Trans Fat | — | — | Vitamin D | 0.7 mcg | 4% |
| Cholesterol | 130 mg | 43% | Potassium | 105 mg | 2% |
| Sodium | 190 mg | 8% | Calcium | 213 mg | 15% |
| Total Carbohydrates | 17 g | 6% | Iron | 1.8 mg | 10% |

# Broccoli & Pork Latkes

**Servings: 4**

**PREP TIME:** 10 minutes | **COOK TIME:** 20 minutes | **TOTAL TIME:** 30 minutes

Level 3: Moderate

This meal has all the nutrients you could ask for, including fiber and antioxidants from the broccoli and protein from the pork. Crispy on the outside, soft on the inside, these latkes are the perfect recipe to use up any leftovers. If using leftover cooked meat instead of ground pork, just be sure to shred it first!

## INGREDIENTS:

1 cup shredded broccoli

½ cup ground pork

3 tablespoons whole-wheat flour

1 tablespoon Italian seasoning

1 tablespoon dried dill

1 teaspoon salt

2 eggs, beaten

1 teaspoon extra-virgin olive oil

## INSTRUCTIONS:

1. Combine the broccoli and pork in a mixing bowl, then add the flour, Italian seasoning, dill, and salt, mixing until combined.

2. Stir in the eggs, mixing until smooth.

3. Heat the olive oil in a skillet over medium-high heat.

4. Spoon ½ cup of the mixture per latke into the skillet and cook for 4 minutes on each side, or until golden.

5. Drain the latkes on paper towels, then serve!

| NUTRITION · per one serving · % of Daily Value | | | | | |
|---|---|---|---|---|---|
| Calories | 120 | | Dietary Fiber | 1 g | 4% |
| Total Fat | 7 g | 9% | Total Sugars | — | — |
| Saturated Fat | 2 g | 10% | Protein | 8 g | 16% |
| Polyunsaturated Fat | 0.8 g | — | Vitamin A | 139 mcg | 15% |
| Monounsaturated Fat | 3.1 g | — | Vitamin C | 2.5 mcg | 2% |
| Trans Fat | — | — | Vitamin D | 0.52 mcg | 2% |
| Cholesterol | 70 mg | 23% | Potassium | 152 mg | 4% |
| Sodium | 200 mg | 9% | Calcium | 52 mg | 4% |
| Total Carbohydrates | 8 g | 3% | Iron | 1.5 mg | 8% |

# Pasta Frittata

**Servings: 3**

**PREP TIME:** 15 minutes | **COOK TIME:** 15 minutes | **TOTAL TIME:** 30 minutes

Level 3: Moderate

If you have leftover pasta of any kind, this is the recipe you'll want to reference! This dish is endlessly versatile, 100 percent foolproof, and good for you, too. Eggs are a good source of protein, heart-healthy unsaturated fats, and important nutrients, such as vitamins $B_6$, $B_{12}$, and D. Whole milk is also loaded with essential nutrients including vitamin D, phosphorous, calcium, B *vitamins*, and protein. Moreover, it may help inhibit osteoporosis, prevent bone fractures, and help you regulate your weight. Don't be afraid to experiment by substituting your own favorite cheeses and seasonings for the cheddar and spices below. There's simply no way to mess this one up!

## INGREDIENTS:

1 cup whole milk

3 eggs, beaten

2 ounces cheddar cheese, shredded

1 teaspoon salt

1 teaspoon chopped fresh dill

¼ teaspoon crushed red pepper flakes

¼ teaspoon paprika

¼ teaspoon ground black pepper

2 ounces cooked tagliatelle pasta or linguine pasta (follow package instructions and cook to al dente)

1 teaspoon extra-virgin olive oil

## INSTRUCTIONS:

1. Preheat the oven to 360°F.

2. Whisk together the milk, eggs, cheese, salt, dill, red pepper flakes, paprika, and pepper in a large bowl. Using a spatula, mix in the cooked pasta.

3. Coat an oven-safe skillet with the olive oil, then pour the frittata batter into the skillet and spread it into an even layer.

4. Bake for 15 minutes, until golden brown. Remove from the oven, then chill for 10 minutes in the fridge before slicing and serving.

| NUTRITION · per one serving · % of Daily Value | | | | | |
|---|---|---|---|---|---|
| Calories | 230 | | Dietary Fiber | 1 g | 3% |
| Total Fat | 11 g | 14% | Total Sugars | 6 g | — |
| Saturated Fat | 6.1 g | 31% | Protein | 14 g | 28% |
| Polyunsaturated Fat | 0.5 g | — | Vitamin A | 222 mcg | 25% |
| Monounsaturated Fat | 3.9 g | — | Vitamin C | 11.9 mcg | 15% |
| *Trans* Fat | — | — | Vitamin D | 3.35 mcg | 15% |
| Cholesterol | 25 mg | 8% | Potassium | 551 mg | 10% |
| Sodium | 190 mg | 8% | Calcium | 351 mg | 25% |
| Total Carbohydrates | 18 g | 7% | Iron | 0.8 mg | 4% |

GF
SF
EF
NF
VE

# Stuffed Portobello Mushrooms

**Servings: 4**

**PREP TIME:** 10 minutes | **COOK TIME:** 15 minutes | **TOTAL TIME:** 25 minutes

Level 3: Moderate

These creamy stuffed mushroom caps are ideal for busy days when you don't have much time in the kitchen. Chock-full of vitamin D, protein, and antioxidants, this meal pairs well with the Simple Mediterranean Salad (page 168) on a cool winter evening or the Watermelon & Feta Salad (page 82) on a sweltering summer night.

## INGREDIENTS:

2 Portobello mushrooms

2 tablespoons extra-virgin olive oil

2 ounces artichoke hearts, drained and chopped

1 tablespoon coconut cream

1 tablespoon cream cheese

1 tablespoon chopped fresh cilantro

1 teaspoon minced garlic

1 cup steamed spinach, chopped

3 ounces cheddar cheese, shredded

½ teaspoon salt

½ teaspoon ground black pepper

## INSTRUCTIONS:

1. Preheat the oven to 360°F and line a baking sheet with parchment paper.

2. Drizzle the Portobello mushrooms with olive oil, then place them onto the prepared baking sheet. Bake for 5 minutes, until juices leak out. Remove from the oven.

3. Combine the artichoke hearts, coconut cream, cream cheese, cilantro, and garlic in a large bowl. Mix in the spinach, cheddar cheese, salt, and pepper.

4. Stuff the mushrooms with the cheese mixture and bake for an additional 5–8 minutes, or until the cheese melts. Remove from the oven and allow to cool on the pan for 5 minutes.

5. Cut each mushroom in half and serve.

**NUTRITION** · per one serving · % of Daily Value

| | | | | | | |
|---|---|---|---|---|---|---|
| Calories | 140 | | Dietary Fiber | 2 g | 7% |
| Total Fat | 11 g | 14% | Total Sugars | 2 g | — |
| Saturated Fat | 4 g | 20% | Protein | 6 g | 12% |
| Polyunsaturated Fat | 0.9 g | — | Vitamin A | 290 mcg | 30% |
| Monounsaturated Fat | 5.8 g | — | Vitamin C | 17.2 mg | 20% |
| *Trans* Fat | — | — | Vitamin D | 0.12 mcg | — |
| Cholesterol | 10 mg | 3% | Potassium | 328 mg | 6% |
| Sodium | 360 mg | 16% | Calcium | 136 mg | 10% |
| Total Carbohydrates | 7 g | 3% | Iron | 0.4 mg | 4% |

**GF**
**SF**
**EF**
**NF**

# Garlic Beef Salpicao

**Servings: 2**

**PREP TIME:** 15 minutes | **COOK TIME:** 15 minutes | **TOTAL TIME:** 30 minutes

Level 3: Moderate

This savory dish packs a flavorful punch! Worcestershire sauce, lime juice, and chili peppers co-star with garlic in this *anything*-but-typical steak. Be sure to cook the garlic in warm, not hot, butter to maximize its aroma and infuse the butter with garlicky goodness.

## INGREDIENTS:

1 pound boneless ribeye steak, cut into thin strips

1 tablespoon Worcestershire sauce

1 tablespoon lime juice

½ teaspoon salt

½ teaspoon chili pepper

2 tablespoons unsalted butter

2 garlic cloves, diced

1 tablespoon sour cream

## INSTRUCTIONS:

1. Place the steak strips in a medium mixing bowl and add the Worcestershire sauce, lime juice, salt, and chili powder and massage the mixture into the steak, then set aside to marinate for 15 minutes.

2. Heat the butter in a large skillet over medium-high heat.

3. Add the garlic and cook for 2 minutes. Add the marinated steak and cook for 2 minutes per side, or until it begins to brown.

4. Stir in the sour cream and cover the skillet with a lid. Cook for 10 minutes, stirring occasionally to incorporate all the flavors. Remove from the heat and allow to cool for 3 minutes.

5. Transfer to a platter and serve!

| NUTRITION · per one serving · % of Daily Value | | | | | |
|---|---|---|---|---|---|
| Calories | 390 | | Dietary Fiber | 1 g | 0% |
| Total Fat | 14 g | 18% | Total Sugars | — | — |
| Saturated Fat | 6.2 g | 31% | Protein | 52 g | 104% |
| Polyunsaturated Fat | 0.7 g | — | Vitamin A | 122 mcg | 15% |
| Monounsaturated Fat | 7.3 g | — | Vitamin C | 30.5 mg | 35% |
| *Trans* Fat | — | — | Vitamin D | 0.32 mcg | 2% |
| Cholesterol | 125 mg | 42% | Potassium | 994 mg | 20% |
| Sodium | 540 mg | 23% | Calcium | 35 mg | 2% |
| Total Carbohydrates | 3 g | 1% | Iron | 5.6 mg | 30% |

SF
GF
NF
VE

# Potato Hash with Asparagus, Chickpeas, & Poached Eggs

**Servings: 4**

**PREP TIME:** 5 minutes | **COOK TIME:** 25 minutes | **TOTAL TIME:** 30 minutes

Level 4: Challenging

This beautiful dish has it all—countless nutrients, mouth-watering aromas, and vivid colors. Looking forward to this meal is a guaranteed way to sprinkle a little pep in my step, even on the dreariest of days. And I'm sure all the vitamin A and protein don't hurt, either!

## INGREDIENTS:

3 tablespoons extra-virgin olive oil, divided

2 russet potatoes, diced

1 small yellow onion, chopped

2 garlic cloves, chopped

1 teaspoon salt

½ teaspoon ground black pepper

1 pound baby asparagus, trimmed and finely chopped

1 cup canned chickpeas, drained and rinsed

1½ teaspoons ground allspice

1 teaspoon za'atar

1 teaspoon dried oregano

1 teaspoon sweet or smoked paprika

1 teaspoon ground coriander

## INSTRUCTIONS:

1. Heat 1½ tablespoons of olive oil in a large skillet over medium-high heat.

2. Add the potatoes, onion, garlic, salt, and pepper, and cook, stirring occasionally, for 5–7 minutes, until the potatoes are tender.

3. Stir in the asparagus, chickpeas, allspice, za'atar, oregano, paprika, coriander, and sugar and cook for 5–7 minutes more to incorporate all the flavors.

4. Decrease the heat to medium-low to keep the hash warm while you poach the eggs. Stir occasionally while you proceed with the next steps.

5. Fill a large saucepan with the water and bring to a boil over medium-high heat.

6. Reduce the heat to low and keep the water at a gentle boil. Add the white vinegar to the water and stir in a circular motion to create a vortex at the center of the pot.

7. Carefully crack 1 egg into the center of the vortex and gently stir again to maintain the circular motion while the egg is cooking. Adjust the heat if needed to maintain a gentle boil.

1 teaspoon sugar

5 cups water

1 teaspoon white vinegar

4 eggs

2 Roma tomatoes, chopped

1 small red onion, minced

1 cup freshly chopped parsley leaves

½ cup crumbled feta

Set a timer for 3½ minutes. Once the time is up, carefully scoop the poached egg out of the water then drain on a kitchen towel. Repeat the same process with the remaining eggs.

8. Transfer the potato hash from the skillet to a serving dish, add the tomatoes, red onion, parsley, and feta, and top with the poached eggs. Serve and enjoy!

| NUTRITION · per one serving · % of Daily Value | | | | | |
|---|---|---|---|---|---|
| Calories | 340 | | Dietary Fiber | 9 g | 32% |
| Total Fat | 13 g | 17% | Total Sugars | 7 g | — |
| Saturated Fat | 4.9 g | 25% | Protein | 18 g | 36% |
| Polyunsaturated Fat | 2.1 g | — | Vitamin A | 998 mcg | 110% |
| Monounsaturated Fat | 5.2 g | — | Vitamin C | 43.5 mcg | 50% |
| Trans Fat | — | — | Vitamin D | 0.9 mcg | 4% |
| Cholesterol | 110 mg | 37% | Potassium | 1086 mg | 25% |
| Sodium | 160 mg | 7% | Calcium | 223 mg | 15% |
| Total Carbohydrates | 40 g | 15% | Iron | 6.7 mg | 35% |

# DINNER

GF
VG
SF
EF
NF
DF

# Mediterranean Bowl

**Servings: 1**

**PREP TIME:** 5 minutes | **COOK TIME:** 0 minutes | **TOTAL TIME:** 5 minutes

Level 1: Very Easy

If you're in need of a one-hit wonder for a quick weeknight dinner, this is the recipe for you! The timeless Mediterranean ingredients, including summer vegetables, chewy quinoa, tangy olives, and creamy hummus, make this an epic power dinner. Did I mention it only takes five minutes to make?

## INGREDIENTS:

1 small cucumber, cubed

½ cup halved cherry tomatoes

½ cup fresh parsley

⅓ cup canned chickpeas, drained and rinsed

8 olives, pitted

3 tablespoons cooked quinoa

1 tablespoon vinegar

1 teaspoon extra-virgin olive oil

½ teaspoon ground black pepper

2 tablespoons hummus

## INSTRUCTIONS:

1. Combine the cucumber, cherry tomatoes, parsley, chickpeas, olives, and quinoa in a serving bowl.

2. Whisk together the vinegar, olive oil, and black pepper in a small bowl, then drizzle it over the salad. Top with the hummus and serve!

**NUTRITION** · per one serving · % of Daily Value

| | | | | | |
|---|---|---|---|---|---|
| Calories | 341 | | Dietary Fiber | 10 g | 48% |
| Total Fat | 14.2 g | 22% | Total Sugars | 9 g | — |
| Saturated Fat | 1.7 g | 8% | Protein | 11 g | 24% |
| Polyunsaturated Fat | 7.8 g | — | Vitamin A | 355 mcg | 68% |
| Monounsaturated Fat | 5 g | — | Vitamin C | 57 mcg | 96% |
| Trans Fat | — | — | Vitamin D | — | — |
| Cholesterol | — | — | Potassium | 831 mg | 15% |
| Sodium | 247 mg | 27% | Calcium | 154 mg | 12% |
| Total Carbohydrates | 44 g | 15% | Iron | 4.73 mg | 26% |

# Balsamic Chickpea Salad

**Servings: 2**

**PREP TIME:** 10 minutes | **COOK TIME:** 0 minutes | **TOTAL TIME:** 10 minutes

Level 1: Very Easy

This zesty salad has a lot to offer, with a range of textures and flavors including sweet balsamic vinegar, crunchy sesame seeds, fresh basil, and chewy chickpeas. This protein-packed dish is vegan-friendly and gluten-free, which makes it an excellent option for family gatherings!

## INGREDIENTS:

1 (15-oz.) can chickpeas, drained and rinsed

2 large tomatoes, chopped

1 carrot, grated

½ cup chopped cilantro leaves

1 tablespoon extra-virgin olive oil

1 tablespoon balsamic vinegar

1 teaspoon salt

10 basil leaves

2 tablespoons sesame seeds

1 teaspoon sunflower seeds

## INSTRUCTIONS:

1. Combine the chickpeas, tomatoes, carrot, cilantro, olive oil, vinegar, and salt in a serving bowl, tossing to combine.

2. Garnish with the basil leaves, sesame seeds, and sunflower seeds, then serve!

| NUTRITION · per one serving · % of Daily Value | | | | | |
|---|---|---|---|---|---|
| Calories | 416 | | Dietary Fiber | 12 g | 49% |
| Total Fat | 16.4 g | 25% | Total Sugars | 12 g | — |
| Saturated Fat | 2.1 g | 10% | Protein | 13 g | 26% |
| Polyunsaturated Fat | 1 g | — | Vitamin A | 1923 mcg | 141% |
| Monounsaturated Fat | 1 g | — | Vitamin C | 28.4 mcg | 47% |
| Trans Fat | — | — | Vitamin D | — | — |
| Cholesterol | — | — | Potassium | 759 mg | 13% |
| Sodium | 630 mg | 15% | Calcium | 99 mg | 10% |
| Total Carbohydrates | 48 g | 13% | Iron | 2.73 mg | 15% |

**GF**
**EF**
**VE**
**NF**
**SF**

# Greek Quinoa Salad

**Servings: 2**

**PREP TIME:** 10 minutes | **COOK TIME:** 0 minutes | **TOTAL TIME:** 10 minutes

Level 1: Very Easy

I love experimenting in the kitchen, but every once in a while, even I feel uninspired. Thankfully, I whipped this up when I was in a salad rut, and it's become a family favorite! Perfect for dinner on a sizzling summer evening or served as an appetizer, this dish does not disappoint.

## INGREDIENTS:

1 cup cooked quinoa

1 cup halved cherry tomatoes

1 cup chopped roasted cauliflower

1 cup arugula

1 roasted red pepper, chopped

3 tablespoons crumbled feta cheese

1 garlic clove, minced

2 tablespoons extra-virgin olive oil

1 tablespoon lemon juice

## INSTRUCTIONS:

1. Combine the quinoa, tomatoes, cauliflower, arugula, roasted red pepper, feta, garlic, olive oil, and lemon juice in a large bowl, tossing to combine.

2. Divide between two bowls and serve!

| NUTRITION · per one serving · % of Daily Value | | | | | |
|---|---|---|---|---|---|
| Calories | 341 | | Dietary Fiber | 6 g | 22% |
| Total Fat | 21.3 g | 33% | Total Sugars | 7 g | — |
| Saturated Fat | 6 g | 30% | Protein | 10 g | 20% |
| Polyunsaturated Fat | 2.8 g | — | Vitamin A | 388 mcg | 41% |
| Monounsaturated Fat | 11.5 g | — | Vitamin C | 105 mcg | 175% |
| Trans Fat | — | — | Vitamin D | 0.1 mcg | 1% |
| Cholesterol | 23 mg | 8% | Potassium | 551 mg | 11% |
| Sodium | 344 mg | 14% | Calcium | 181 mg | 18% |
| Total Carbohydrates | 29.8 g | 10% | Iron | 2.36 mg | 13% |

GF
DF
 EF
VG
SF
NF

# Vegan Avocado & Chickpea Salad

**Servings: 2**

**PREP TIME:** 5 minutes | **COOK TIME:** 0 minutes | **TOTAL TIME:** 5 minutes

Level 1: Very Easy

Every week my family participates in meat-free Mondays. I truly believe reducing our consumption of animal products helps the environment. And at the same time, it gets my creative juices flowing! This recipe, which I created for one such meatless Monday, is packed with vitamins and essential nutrients, and one serving surpasses your daily-recommended intake of fiber!

## INGREDIENTS:

2 cups cooked chickpeas, peeled

1 cup chopped tomatoes

1 avocado, cubed

1 carrot, peeled and julienned

6 basil leaves

1 tablespoon extra-virgin olive oil

1 teaspoon lemon juice

½ teaspoon salt

½ teaspoon ground black pepper

1 teaspoon toasted sesame seeds

## INSTRUCTIONS:

1. Combine the chickpeas, tomatoes, avocado, carrot, basil, olive oil, lemon juice, salt, and pepper in a medium bowl, tossing to combine.

2. Divide between two serving bowls and garnish with the toasted sesame seeds. Serve and enjoy!

| NUTRITION · per one serving · % of Daily Value | | | | | |
|---|---|---|---|---|---|
| Calories | 946 | | Dietary Fiber | 30.41 g | 109% |
| Total Fat | 28.36 g | 40% | Total Sugars | 25.50 g | — |
| Saturated Fat | 3.52 g | 18% | Protein | 43.52 g | 87% |
| Polyunsaturated Fat | 7.6 g | — | Vitamin A | 321 mcg | 23% |
| Monounsaturated Fat | 15.7 g | — | Vitamin C | 29.13 mcg | 36% |
| Trans Fat | — | — | Vitamin D | — | — |
| Cholesterol | — | — | Potassium | 2032.1 mg | 58% |
| Sodium | 657.48 mg | 33% | Calcium | 150.19 mg | 19% |
| Total Carbohydrates | 137.32 g | 53% | Iron | 9.57 mg | 68% |

# Quick Chickpea Bruschetta

**Servings: 2**

**PREP TIME:** 5 minutes | **COOK TIME:** 0 minutes | **TOTAL TIME:** 5 minutes

Level 1: Very Easy

So, your friends were supposed to show up in the evening, but appeared at 3 p.m.? With this speedy recipe in your back pocket, you don't have to waste socializing time in the kitchen! And thanks to the protein-packed chickpeas, this dish can regulate blood sugar, reduce cholesterol, and boost brain function.

## INGREDIENTS:

1 cup canned chickpeas, drained and rinsed

1 medium tomato, chopped

½ cup chopped fresh basil

1 garlic clove, minced

1 tablespoon extra-virgin olive oil

1 teaspoon tomato paste

½ teaspoon ground cumin

2 slices whole-wheat bread, toasted

## INSTRUCTIONS:

1. Combine the chickpeas, tomatoes, basil, garlic, olive oil, tomato paste, and cumin in a bowl, tossing to combine.

2. Place the mixture on the slices of toasted bread and serve.

**NUTRITION** · per one serving · % of Daily Value

| | | | | | |
|---|---|---|---|---|---|
| Calories | 386 | | Dietary Fiber | 11 g | 43% |
| Total Fat | 18.3 g | 28% | Total Sugars | 10 g | 15% |
| Saturated Fat | 2.3 g | 12% | Protein | 13 g | 26% |
| Polyunsaturated Fat | 3.1 g | — | Vitamin A | 372 mcg | 36% |
| Monounsaturated Fat | 10.7 g | — | Vitamin C | 21.4 mcg | 36% |
| Trans Fat | — | — | Vitamin D | — | — |
| Cholesterol | — | — | Potassium | 178 mg | 13% |
| Sodium | 422 mg | 18% | Calcium | 137 mg | 14% |
| Total Carbohydrates | 46 g | 15% | Iron | 3.8 mg | 21% |

# No-Cook Tuna & Bean Wraps

**Servings: 4**

**PREP TIME:** 10 minutes | **COOK TIME:** 0 minutes | **TOTAL TIME:** 10 minutes

Level 2: Easy

No-cook wraps are every busy bee's dream! Whether you care for children or work full-time, time always flies on weeknights. This fiber- and protein-rich meal can be assembled in just ten minutes to silence your hunger pangs, all while tasting delicious.

## INGREDIENTS:

1 (15-oz.) can cannellini beans, drained and rinsed

1 (4-oz.) can light tuna in water, drained and flaked with a fork

2 tablespoons extra-virgin olive oil

1 tablespoon fresh parsley

⅛ teaspoon salt

⅛ teaspoon pepper

4 (8-inch) whole-wheat tortillas

1 ripe avocado, sliced

## INSTRUCTIONS:

1. Combine the beans, tuna, olive oil, parsley, salt, and pepper in a small bowl, tossing to mix.

2. Warm the tortillas in the microwave for 10 seconds and place each one on a plate.

3. Divide the bean–tuna mixture among the four tortillas and roll each into a wrap. Top each tortilla wrap with slices of avocado. Serve and enjoy!

| NUTRITION · per one serving · % of Daily Value | | | | | |
|---|---|---|---|---|---|
| Calories | 353 | | Dietary Fiber | 10 g | 41% |
| Total Fat | 15.51 g | 24% | Total Sugars | 1 g | — |
| Saturated Fat | 2.3 g | 12% | Protein | 26.2 g | 52% |
| Polyunsaturated Fat | 2.1 g | — | Vitamin A | 361 mcg | 34% |
| Monounsaturated Fat | 9.9 g | — | Vitamin C | 12.4 mcg | 21% |
| Trans Fat | — | — | Vitamin D | 8 mcg | 6% |
| Cholesterol | 28 mg | 9% | Potassium | 856 mg | 18% |
| Sodium | 829 mg | 35% | Calcium | 95 mg | 10% |
| Total Carbohydrates | 30.61 g | 10% | Iron | 4.51 mg | 25% |

VE
NF
EF
SF
GF

# Greek Mixed Greens

**Servings: 2**

**PREP TIME:** 5 minutes | **COOK TIME:** 0 minutes | **TOTAL TIME:** 5 minutes

Level 1: Very Easy

It may be crafted with traditional Mediterranean flavors—including fresh tomatoes, salty feta, and robust red-wine vinegar—but this salad is anything but ordinary. Serve it alone for a light dinner or as a side with Italian Chicken Wraps (page 156) or Baked Lemon Salmon (page 248).

## INGREDIENTS:

2 cups arugula

⅓ cup cherry tomatoes

⅓ cup diced cucumber

1½ tablespoons extra-virgin olive oil

2 teaspoons red-wine vinegar

¼ teaspoon ground cumin

⅛ teaspoon ground pepper

1 tablespoon crumbled feta cheese

1 tablespoon sunflower seeds

## INSTRUCTIONS:

1. Combine the arugula, tomatoes, cucumber, olive oil, vinegar, cumin, and pepper in a medium bowl, tossing to mix.

2. Top with the feta and sunflower seeds, then serve.

**NUTRITION** · per one serving · % of Daily Value

| | | | | | |
|---|---|---|---|---|---|
| Calories | 147.3 | | Dietary Fiber | 1.16 g | 4% |
| Total Fat | 14.21 g | 20% | Total Sugars | 1.53 g | — |
| Saturated Fat | 2.33 g | 12% | Protein | 2.51 g | 5% |
| Polyunsaturated Fat | 2.26 g | — | Vitamin A | 287 mcg | 30% |
| Monounsaturated Fat | 8.88 g | — | Vitamin C | 15 mcg | 15% |
| Trans Fat | 0.003 g | — | Vitamin D | 0.4 mcg | 2% |
| Cholesterol | 4.17 mg | 1% | Potassium | 202.76 mg | 6% |
| Sodium | 61.9 mg | 3% | Calcium | 67.7 mg | 8% |
| Total Carbohydrates | 3.73 g | 1% | Iron | 0.95 mg | 7% |

NF
EF
SF

# Italian Salami Sandwich

**Servings: 4**

**PREP TIME:** 5 minutes | **COOK TIME:** 0 minutes | **TOTAL TIME:** 5 minutes

Level 2: Easy

You'll never visit another sandwich shop after biting into this creation! Cypriot is a special kind of salami made from meat that has *been* soaked in red wine and salt, then spiced with cumin, pepper, and coriander. Here it's paired with sharp green onion and creamy mascarpone cheese for an irresistible spicy-sweet combination.

## INGREDIENTS:

8 ounces mascarpone cheese

½ cup torn basil leaves

¼ cup chopped green onions

1 garlic clove, minced

8 slices whole-wheat bread

4 large leaves of lettuce

10 ounces Cypriot salami or sausage

## INSTRUCTIONS:

1. Combine the mascarpone cheese, basil, green onions, and garlic in a small bowl, tossing thoroughly to mix.

2. Spread 2 tablespoons of the mascarpone mixture onto one side of each bread slice.

3. Layer the lettuce and salami onto four bread slices and top with the remaining bread slices. Serve and enjoy!

| NUTRITION · per one serving · % of Daily Value | | | | | |
|---|---|---|---|---|---|
| Calories | 582 | | Dietary Fiber | 5 g | 19% |
| Total Fat | 43 g | 65% | Total Sugars | 5 g | — |
| Saturated Fat | 17.6 g | 88% | Protein | 24 g | 48% |
| Polyunsaturated Fat | 6.2 g | — | Vitamin A | 1053 mcg | 53% |
| Monounsaturated Fat | 16 g | — | Vitamin C | 20 mcg | 35% |
| *Trans* Fat | 0.3 g | — | Vitamin D | 2 mcg | 7% |
| Cholesterol | 139 mg | 46% | Potassium | 635 mg | 14% |
| Sodium | 1687 mg | 70% | Calcium | 123 mg | 12% |
| Total Carbohydrates | 36 g | 13% | Iron | 3.51 mg | 20% |

# Vegan Lebanese Fatteh

EF
DF
VG
SF

**Servings: 4**

**PREP TIME:** 10 minutes | **COOK TIME:** 0 minutes | **TOTAL TIME:** 10 minutes

Level 2: Easy

Fatteh is a traditional Levantine dish, also known as fette, fatta, or fetté. In Egypt, the dish is reserved for special occasions, like celebrating a woman's first pregnancy or an evening meal for Muslims to break their Ramadan fast. Iron- and protein-rich, this classic dish takes just ten minutes to make.

## INGREDIENTS:

1 cup tahini

1 garlic clove, minced

2 teaspoons lemon juice

¼ tablespoon kosher salt

1 (15-oz.) can chickpeas, drained and rinsed

¼ cup cashews, toasted

1 teaspoon sumac

2 (6-inch) pitas, toasted and cut into 1-inch pieces

## INSTRUCTIONS:

1. Whisk together the tahini, garlic, lemon juice, and salt in a small bowl.

2. Combine the chickpeas, cashews, and sumac in a medium bowl, tossing well.

3. Divide the chickpea mixture among four bowls, then add the pita chips on top.

4. Top with the tahini dressing and serve.

**NUTRITION** · per one serving · % of Daily Value

| | | | | | |
|---|---|---|---|---|---|
| Calories | 500 | | Dietary Fiber | 11 g | 45% |
| Total Fat | 40 g | 60% | Total Sugars | 4 g | — |
| Saturated Fat | 5 g | 29% | Protein | 17 g | 34% |
| Polyunsaturated Fat | 17 g | — | Vitamin A | — | 1% |
| Monounsaturated Fat | 16 g | — | Vitamin C | 1.3 mcg | 2% |
| Trans Fat | — | — | Vitamin D | 0.4 mcg | 2% |
| Cholesterol | — | — | Potassium | 429 mg | 9% |
| Sodium | 625 mg | 26% | Calcium | 298 mg | 30% |
| Total Carbohydrates | 35 g | 12% | Iron | 7.2 mg | 40% |

**NF** **EF** **DF** **GF**

# Grilled Chicken & Vegetable Salad

**Servings: 1**

**PREP TIME:** 5 minutes | **COOK TIME:** 0 minutes | **TOTAL TIME:** 5 minutes

Level 3: Moderate

A hearty salad is my favorite for a satisfying dinner on a warm summer evening. If you ever struggle with getting your kids to eat their fair share of veggies, they'll devour this dish! The variety of textures, flavors, and colors is guaranteed to pique their interest.

## INGREDIENTS:

1 cup chopped grilled zucchini

¾ cups shredded grilled chicken

1 large potato, baked and sliced

¼ cup chopped grilled tomatoes

1 tablespoon balsamic vinegar

1 teaspoon extra-virgin olive oil

1 tablespoon sunflower seeds

## INSTRUCTIONS:

1. Combine the zucchini, chicken, potato, and tomatoes in a bowl, tossing well.

2. Drizzle the vinegar and olive oil on top and garnish with the sunflower seeds. Serve and enjoy!

| NUTRITION · per one serving · % of Daily Value | | | | | |
|---|---|---|---|---|---|
| Calories | 448 | | Dietary Fiber | 6 g | 23% |
| Total Fat | 14.05 g | 22% | Total Sugars | 8 g | — |
| Saturated Fat | 2.3 g | 11% | Protein | 36.8 g | 74% |
| Polyunsaturated Fat | 3.7 g | — | Vitamin A | 53 mcg | 5% |
| Monounsaturated Fat | 6.5 g | — | Vitamin C | 34.7 mcg | 58% |
| Trans Fat | — | — | Vitamin D | 0.1 mcg | 1% |
| Cholesterol | 79 mg | 26% | Potassium | 480 mg | 39% |
| Sodium | 110 mg | 5% | Calcium | 57 mg | 6% |
| Total Carbohydrates | 44 g | 15% | Iron | 4.27 mg | 24% |

# Lebanese Lettuce Wraps

**VG** **EF** **DF** **GF** **SF**

**Servings: 4**

**PREP TIME:** 10 minutes | **COOK TIME:** 0 minutes | **TOTAL TIME:** 10 minutes

Level 2: Easy

This nutritious, meatless, and fiber-packed recipe makes the perfect filling dinner. Earthy chickpeas seasoned with bright lemon zest, fruity paprika, and nutty tahini elevate otherwise bland lettuce wraps into a wonderfully delightful vegan-friendly meal.

## INGREDIENTS:

¼ cup tahini

¼ cup fresh lemon juice

1 teaspoon lemon zest

¾ teaspoon salt

½ teaspoon ground paprika

1 cup canned chickpeas, drained and rinsed

½ cup canned roasted red peppers, drained and sliced

4 large iceberg lettuce leaves

¼ cup chopped toasted walnuts

2 tablespoons fresh parsley leaves

## INSTRUCTIONS:

1. Whisk together the tahini, lemon juice, lemon zest, salt, and paprika in a medium bowl.

2. Add the chickpeas and roasted red peppers, tossing to combine.

3. Arrange the lettuce leaves on a serving platter. Add ⅓ cup of the chickpea mixture to each one and top with walnuts and parsley. Fold the lettuce over the filling to seal it.

4. Serve and enjoy!

| NUTRITION · per one serving · % of Daily Value | | | | | |
|---|---|---|---|---|---|
| Calories | 498 | | Dietary Fiber | 9.6 g | 36% |
| Total Fat | 28 g | 36% | Total Sugars | 4 g | — |
| Saturated Fat | 3.5 g | 18% | Protein | 15.8 g | 32% |
| Polyunsaturated Fat | 9.4 g | — | Vitamin A | 127 mcg | 15% |
| Monounsaturated Fat | 8.5 g | — | Vitamin C | 8.6 mcg | 10% |
| *Trans* Fat | 0.001 g | — | Vitamin D | 0.2 mcg | — |
| Cholesterol | 42 mg | 13% | Potassium | 620 mg | 15% |
| Sodium | 567 mg | 25% | Calcium | 162 mg | 16% |
| Total Carbohydrates | 43.7 g | 16% | Iron | 4 mg | 20% |

# Vegan Lentil & Kale Salad

**Servings: 4**

**PREP TIME:** 15 minutes | **COOK TIME:** 0 minutes | **TOTAL TIME:** 15 minutes

Level 1: Very Easy

This plant-powered recipe draws inspiration from the Mediterranean, with tangy sun-dried tomatoes, sour apple cider vinegar, and hearty lentils. Lentils are one of your pantry's most humble and underrated items; quick-cooking and fiber-rich, these legumes are the star of this salad!

## INGREDIENTS:

¼ purple cabbage, finely diced

1 tablespoon chopped sun-dried tomatoes

1 garlic clove, minced

¼ cup apple cider vinegar

2 tablespoons extra-virgin olive oil

½ teaspoon Dijon mustard

¼ teaspoon salt

¼ teaspoon ground black pepper

8 cups finely chopped kale

1 (9-oz.) package refrigerated and pre-cooked lentils, steamed

## INSTRUCTIONS:

1. Whisk together the cabbage, sun-dried tomatoes, garlic, vinegar, olive oil, mustard, salt, and pepper in a large bowl.

2. Add the kale and lentils, tossing well to combine. Serve and enjoy!

**NUTRITION** · per one serving · % of Daily Value

| | | | | | |
|---|---|---|---|---|---|
| Calories | 186 | | Dietary Fiber | 7.4 g | 25% |
| Total Fat | 8.6 g | 12% | Total Sugars | 3.2 g | — |
| Saturated Fat | 1.8 g | 9% | Protein | 9.6 g | 18% |
| Polyunsaturated Fat | 0.5 g | — | Vitamin A | 789 mcg | 90% |
| Monounsaturated Fat | 3.1 g | — | Vitamin C | 49 mcg | 50% |
| Trans Fat | — | — | Vitamin D | 2 mcg | 10% |
| Cholesterol | 3.6 mg | 1% | Potassium | 376 mg | 8% |
| Sodium | 464.1 mg | 20% | Calcium | 215.8 mg | 15% |
| Total Carbohydrates | 18.2 g | 7% | Iron | 3.6 mg | 3.6% |

# Tuna & Artichoke Salad

**Servings: 1**

**PREP TIME:** 10 minutes | **COOK TIME:** 0 minutes | **TOTAL TIME:** 10 minutes

Level 1: Very Easy

The tried-and-true tuna salad gets a much-needed upgrade with this recipe. Vitamin C-packed spinach blended with antioxidant-rich artichoke hearts and tuna chock-full of protein make this dinner one of the most nutritious options out there! If you're in the mood to play around, sprinkle in some seeds and nuts for added crunch.

## INGREDIENTS:

1½ tablespoons tahini

1½ tablespoons lemon juice

1½ tablespoons water

1 (5-oz.) can light tuna in water, drained

½ cup chopped artichoke hearts

4 black olives, pitted and chopped

2 tablespoons chopped fresh parsley

2 cups baby spinach

## INSTRUCTIONS:

1. Whisk together the tahini, lemon juice, and water in a medium bowl.

2. Add the tuna, artichokes, olives, and parsley, stirring to combine.

3. Place the spinach leaves in a serving bowl and top with the tuna mixture. Serve and enjoy!

| NUTRITION · per one serving · % of Daily Value | | | | | |
|---|---|---|---|---|---|
| Calories | 376 | | Dietary Fiber | 5.8 g | 21% |
| Total Fat | 21 g | 27% | Total Sugars | 13 g | — |
| Saturated Fat | 5.2 g | 26% | Protein | 25.7 g | 52% |
| Polyunsaturated Fat | 3.1 g | — | Vitamin A | 1774 mcg | 200% |
| Monounsaturated Fat | 6.8 g | — | Vitamin C | 94 mcg | 100% |
| Trans Fat | — | — | Vitamin D | 12 mcg | 60% |
| Cholesterol | 46.3 mg | 15% | Potassium | 779.8 mg | 15% |
| Sodium | 664 mg | 29% | Calcium | 271 mg | 32% |
| Total Carbohydrates | 26.2 g | 9% | Iron | 4.8 mg | 60% |

**NF**
**EF**
**GF**
**VG**
**DF**

# Cauliflower Tabbouleh

**Servings: 2**

**PREP TIME:** 10 minutes | **COOK TIME:** 0 minutes | **TOTAL TIME:** 10 minutes

Level 1: Very Easy

Tabbouleh, made with chopped parsley, is a common appetizer in the Middle East. Dating back to the Middle Ages, this salad grew in popularity as knowledge of edible herbs spread. In this recipe, we pair the traditional ingredients with cauliflower for added satisfaction.

## INGREDIENTS:

4 cups cooked cauliflower rice, warm

2 cups chopped fresh parsley

8 ounces cherry tomatoes, halved

4 green onions, sliced

Zest of 2 lemons

Juice of 2 lemons

¼ cup extra-virgin olive oil

1 tablespoon pomegranate molasses

1 tablespoon dried mint

1 teaspoon sumac

1 teaspoon salt

## INSTRUCTIONS:

1. Combine all the ingredients in a medium bowl and toss to mix.

2. Serve and enjoy!

**NUTRITION** · per one serving · % of Daily Value

| | | | | | |
|---|---|---|---|---|---|
| Calories | 365 | | Dietary Fiber | 7 g | 28% |
| Total Fat | 28.3 g | 44% | Total Sugars | 16 g | — |
| Saturated Fat | 4 g | 20% | Protein | 6.1 g | 12% |
| Polyunsaturated Fat | 3 g | — | Vitamin A | 1726 mcg | 142% |
| Monounsaturated Fat | 19 g | — | Vitamin C | 188 mcg | 314% |
| Trans Fat | 0.013 g | — | Vitamin D | — | — |
| Cholesterol | — | — | Potassium | 1288 mg | 20% |
| Sodium | 93 mg | 4% | Calcium | 168 mg | 17% |
| Total Carbohydrates | 27.9 g | 9% | Iron | 5.7 mg | 32% |

# Greek Vegetarian Bowl

**Servings: 4**

**PREP TIME:** 10 minutes | **COOK TIME:** 0 minutes | **TOTAL TIME:** 10 minutes

Level 1: Very Easy

In just ten minutes, you can whip up this satisfying Greek Vegetarian Bowl. While the recipe calls for vegetables of your choosing, I recommend a mix of olives, tomatoes, cucumbers, and red onions. As I always say, the more closely it resembles a rainbow, the better!

## INGREDIENTS:

3 cups cooked quinoa

2 cups mixed vegetables, cooked and chopped

1 (15-oz.) can chickpeas, drained and rinsed

½ cup Greek yogurt

Juice of 1 lemon

1 tablespoon extra-virgin olive oil

1 teaspoon ground turmeric

## INSTRUCTIONS:

1. Combine all the ingredients in a medium bowl, tossing to mix.

2. Serve and enjoy!

| NUTRITION · per one serving · % of Daily Value | | | | | |
|---|---|---|---|---|---|
| Calories | 306 | | Dietary Fiber | 10 g | 36% |
| Total Fat | 7.4 g | 9% | Total Sugars | 7.7 g | — |
| Saturated Fat | 0.4 g | 2% | Protein | 11.9 g | 24% |
| Polyunsaturated Fat | 4 g | — | Vitamin A | 812 mcg | 90% |
| Monounsaturated Fat | 2 g | — | Vitamin C | 72 mcg | 80% |
| Trans Fat | — | — | Vitamin D | 0.8 mcg | 4% |
| Cholesterol | 13 mg | 5% | Potassium | 250 mg | 6% |
| Sodium | 148.4 mg | 7% | Calcium | 75.7 mg | 6% |
| Total Carbohydrates | 47.7 g | 17% | Iron | 3 mg | 15% |

# Honey Mustard Bean Salad

**Servings: 4**

**PREP TIME:** 10 minutes | **COOK TIME:** 0 minutes | **TOTAL TIME:** 10 minutes

Level 1: Very Easy

With mixed greens and beans tossed in luscious honey, tangy mustard, and sharp red wine vinegar, this fiber-rich dish is perfect for all seasons. If it's a frosty winter evening and you're in need of a comforting, hearty dinner, flip to this page—or bring this salad to an outdoor gathering and you'll return with an empty bowl, every time!

## INGREDIENTS:

¼ cup olive oil

3 tablespoons red wine vinegar

2 teaspoons Dijon mustard

1 teaspoon raw honey

¼ teaspoon salt

¼ teaspoon ground pepper

10 cups mixed salad greens

1 (15-oz.) can cannellini beans, drained and rinsed

1 cup halved cherry tomatoes

## INSTRUCTIONS:

1. Whisk together the olive oil, red wine vinegar, Dijon mustard, honey, salt, and pepper in a medium bowl. Add the mixed greens, cannellini beans, and tomatoes, tossing to combine.

2. Serve and enjoy!

| NUTRITION · per one serving · % of Daily Value | | | | | |
|---|---|---|---|---|---|
| Calories | 246 | | Dietary Fiber | 7.6 g | 29% |
| Total Fat | 15.3 g | 19% | Total Sugars | 4.9 g | — |
| Saturated Fat | 2 g | 10% | Protein | 7.5 g | 16% |
| Polyunsaturated Fat | 4 g | — | Vitamin A | 912 mcg | 100% |
| Monounsaturated Fat | 1 g | — | Vitamin C | 29.9 mcg | 35% |
| Trans Fat | 2.1 g | — | Vitamin D | 18 mcg | 92% |
| Cholesterol | — | — | Potassium | 793 mg | 15% |
| Sodium | 270 mg | 12% | Calcium | 125.6 mg | 11% |
| Total Carbohydrates | 21.5 g | 8% | Iron | 3.6 mg | 20% |

# Marinated Olive Wraps

**Servings: 3**

**PREP TIME:** 10 minutes | **COOK TIME:** 0 minutes | **TOTAL TIME:** 10 minutes

Level 2: Easy

If you're in a rush, this recipe will take just ten minutes. If you've got the time, I recommend making the olives ahead and letting them marinate in the aromatic rosemary–garlic oil for optimal flavor. While I call for green olives, feel free to substitute your favorite.

## INGREDIENTS:

1½ cups pitted and sliced green olives

2 garlic cloves, minced

2 tablespoons lemon juice

1 tablespoon extra-virgin olive oil

1 teaspoon chopped fresh rosemary

1 teaspoon ground oregano

½ teaspoon crushed red pepper flakes

3 (8-inch) whole-wheat pitas

1 cup arugula leaves

½ cup fresh mint leaves

## INSTRUCTIONS:

1. Combine the green olives, garlic, lemon juice, olive oil, rosemary, red pepper flakes and oregano in a medium bowl.

2. If time allows, cover with a tea towel or plastic wrap and set aside for 1 hour. If you're unable to wait, skip to step 3.

3. Divide the marinated olives among the 3 pitas and top with the arugula and mint. Roll each pita into a burrito and serve!

**NUTRITION** · per one serving · % of Daily Value

| | | | | | |
|---|---|---|---|---|---|
| Calories | 200 | | Dietary Fiber | 5 g | 14% |
| Total Fat | 19 g | 20% | Total Sugars | — | — |
| Saturated Fat | 2.5 g | 13% | Protein | 2 g | 2% |
| Polyunsaturated Fat | 1.4 g | — | Vitamin A | 0.7 mcg | 6% |
| Monounsaturated Fat | 13.2 g | — | Vitamin C | 23 mcg | 2% |
| Trans Fat | 0.002 g | — | Vitamin D | — | — |
| Cholesterol | — | — | Potassium | 30 mg | — |
| Sodium | 1420 mg | 38% | Calcium | 27 mg | 2% |
| Total Carbohydrates | 6 g | 2% | Iron | 0.31 mg | 2% |

# Herbed Labneh Wraps

**Servings: 4**

**PREP TIME:** 10 minutes | **COOK TIME:** 0 minutes | **TOTAL TIME:** 10 minutes

Level 1: Very Easy

If you've never tried labneh before, you're in for a treat! The spread is made by straining yogurt, resulting in a thicker texture, all while preserving the unique flavor. Serve these wraps as a light dinner or pair with Moroccan Chicken (page 236) or Italian Beef Skewers (page 222) for a hearty meal!

## INGREDIENTS:

2 cups labneh

½ cup torn fresh basil

3 garlic cloves, minced

1 tablespoon extra-virgin olive oil

1 tablespoon dried mint

4 (8-inch) whole-wheat pitas

1 cup halved cherry tomatoes

1 tablespoon fresh spearmint

## INSTRUCTIONS:

1. Mix the labneh, basil, garlic, olive oil, and mint together in a bowl until creamy.

2. Spread the herbed labneh onto the pitas and top with the tomatoes and spearmint, then roll each one into a burrito. Serve and enjoy!

| NUTRITION · per one serving · % of Daily Value | | | | | |
|---|---|---|---|---|---|
| Calories | 290 | | Dietary Fiber | — | — |
| Total Fat | 21 g | 27% | Total Sugars | 5 g | — |
| Saturated Fat | 12 g | 60% | Protein | 7 g | 14% |
| Polyunsaturated Fat | 1 g | — | Vitamin A | 2.5 mcg | 15% |
| Monounsaturated Fat | 5.3 g | — | Vitamin C | — | — |
| Trans Fat | 0.9 g | — | Vitamin D | — | — |
| Cholesterol | 60 mg | 20% | Potassium | 126 mg | 2% |
| Sodium | 35 mg | 2% | Calcium | 62 mg | 4% |
| Total Carbohydrates | 6 g | 2% | Iron | 0.25 mg | 2% |

NF
EF
VG
SF
DF

# Vegan Mediterranean Sandwich

**Servings: 1**

**PREP TIME:** 5 minutes | **COOK TIME:** 0 minutes | **TOTAL TIME:** 5 minutes

Level 2: Easy

Reserve this recipe for your first summer harvest! Fresh cucumbers and juicy tomatoes paired with delectable herbs make this sandwich an al fresco dining treat. Better yet, toss this sandwich into your picnic basket and gobble it up with the whole family!

## INGREDIENTS:

4 slices whole-wheat bread, toasted

2 medium tomatoes, sliced

1 large cucumber, sliced

10 spearmint leaves

10 basil leaves

3 tablespoons extra-virgin olive oil

¼ teaspoon salt

⅛ teaspoon pepper

## INSTRUCTIONS

1. To assemble the first layer of the sandwich, place one slice of bread onto a serving plate. Arrange about one-third of the tomato, cucumber, spearmint, and basil on top and add a drizzle of olive oil. Season with a sprinkle of salt and pepper.

2. Top with a second slice of bread and repeat Step 1.

3. Repeat to add a third layer, using up all the remaining filling ingredients, and top with the last piece of bread to create a four-layer sandwich tower! Serve and enjoy.

| NUTRITION · per one serving · % of Daily Value | | | | | |
|---|---|---|---|---|---|
| Calories | 473 | | Dietary Fiber | 6 g | 22% |
| Total Fat | 23.5 g | 36% | Total Sugars | 10 g | — |
| Saturated Fat | 3.4 g | 17% | Protein | 9.4 g | 20% |
| Polyunsaturated Fat | 3.5 g | — | Vitamin A | 386 mcg | 35% |
| Monounsaturated Fat | 15.3 g | — | Vitamin C | 23.4 mcg | 39% |
| Trans Fat | — | — | Vitamin D | — | — |
| Cholesterol | — | — | Potassium | 646 mg | 21% |
| Sodium | 42 mg | 29% | Calcium | 176 mg | 18% |
| Total Carbohydrates | 48.4 g | 16% | Iron | 5.1 mg | 28% |

**NF**
**EF**
**SF**
**VG**
**DF**

# Quick Hummus & Tomato Wrap

**Servings: 1**

**PREP TIME:** 5 minutes | **COOK TIME:** 0 minutes | **TOTAL TIME:** 5 minutes

Level 1: Very Easy

With just six ingredients and ready in five minutes, this recipe makes any weeknight dinner a breeze. If you're interested in pairing it with another dish, I suggest serving alongside Italian Beef Skewers (page 222), or adding some Mediterranean Meatballs (page 244) into your wrap!

## INGREDIENTS:

2 tablespoons hummus

1 (8-inch) whole-wheat pita

½ tablespoon ground cumin

1 teaspoon extra-virgin olive oil

½ cup halved cherry tomatoes

¼ cup chopped fresh mint leaves

## INSTRUCTIONS:

1. Smear the hummus onto the pita bread. Sprinkle the cumin on top and drizzle with the olive oil.

2. Arrange the tomatoes and mint on top and roll the pita into a burrito. Serve and enjoy!

| NUTRITION · per one serving · % of Daily Value | | | | | |
|---|---|---|---|---|---|
| Calories | 202 | | Dietary Fiber | 6 g | 24% |
| Total Fat | 8.8 g | 14% | Total Sugars | 2 g | — |
| Saturated Fat | 1.2 g | 6% | Protein | 6.1 g | 12% |
| Polyunsaturated Fat | 1.6 g | — | Vitamin A | 341 mcg | 32% |
| Monounsaturated Fat | 5.2 g | — | Vitamin C | 15.8 mcg | 26% |
| Trans Fat | — | — | Vitamin D | — | — |
| Cholesterol | — | — | Potassium | 434 mg | 9% |
| Sodium | 213 mg | 9% | Calcium | 100 mg | 10% |
| Total Carbohydrates | 27.5 g | 9% | Iron | 6.2 mg | 35% |

**NF** **EF** **DF** **SF** **GF**

# Italian Zoodle Salad

**Servings: 1**

**PREP TIME:** 10 minutes | **COOK TIME:** 10 minutes | **TOTAL TIME:** 20 minutes

Level 3: Moderate

Sun-dried tomatoes, like many foods throughout history, were originally created as a way to preserve fresh produce and delay its decomposing. Tomatoes were originally salted for preservation; however, Italians began sun-drying tomatoes on ceramic rooftops around the 1900s. Today, these tomatoes add a tangy-tart flavor to meals like this zoodle salad.

## INGREDIENTS:

1 tablespoon extra-virgin olive oil

1 tablespoon lemon juice

¼ cup of water

½ cup sun-dried tomatoes

3 tablespoons sliced olives

1 tablespoon Italian seasoning

1 teaspoon kosher salt

½ teaspoon black ground pepper

4 cups cooked zucchini noodles or julienned zucchini

½ cup sliced cooked chicken, warmed

## INSTRUCTIONS:

1. Whisk together the olive oil, lemon juice, water, sun-dried tomatoes, olives, Italian seasoning, salt, and pepper in a small saucepan.

2. Set the pan over medium-high heat and cook for 10 minutes. When it starts to boil, remove from the heat and transfer to a serving bowl.

3. Add the zucchini noodles and chicken on top. Serve and enjoy!

| NUTRITION · per one serving · % of Daily Value | | | | | |
|---|---|---|---|---|---|
| Calories | 329 | | Dietary Fiber | 4.5 g | 14% |
| Total Fat | 4.5 g | 6% | Total Sugars | 12 g | — |
| Saturated Fat | 4.4 g | 22% | Protein | 24 g | 48% |
| Polyunsaturated Fat | 0.5 g | — | Vitamin A | 435 mcg | 50% |
| Monounsaturated Fat | 0.3 g | — | Vitamin C | 54.3 mcg | 60% |
| Trans Fat | — | — | Vitamin D | — | — |
| Cholesterol | 64.9 mg | 22% | Potassium | 1026.7 mg | 20% |
| Sodium | 719.7 mg | 31% | Calcium | 178.2 mg | 18% |
| Total Carbohydrates | 16 g | 6% | Iron | 2.4 mg | 15% |

**NF**
**GF**
**SF**
**EF**

# Greek Salmon Bowl

**Servings: 2**

**PREP TIME:** 15 minutes | **COOK TIME:** 15 minutes | **TOTAL TIME:** 30 minutes

Level 3: Moderate

Salmon is a Mediterranean favorite that's loaded with omega-3s, protein, and vitamin $B_{12}$. The key to any flavorful fish is the marinade or rub. Here we use dried basil for some zest, crushed red pepper for a kick, and garlic for a familiar Greek flavor. If you feel like channeling your inner Greek, top with a dollop of tzatziki!

1 teaspoon dried basil

½ teaspoon crushed red pepper flakes

2 garlic cloves, minced, divided

8-ounce salmon fillet

⅔ cup chopped purple cabbage

1 tablespoon lemon juice

1 cup chopped lettuce

¼ cup crumbled feta cheese

Handful of fresh basil

3 tablespoons extra-virgin olive oil, divided

1 cup broccoli florets

½ cup pitted and sliced olives

2 tablespoons hummus

1. Combine the dried basil, crushed red pepper flakes, and half the garlic in a medium bowl, then add the salmon.

2. Massage the herb mixture into the salmon and set aside for 10–15 minutes.

3. Combine the cabbage and lemon juice in a medium bowl, mixing well. Add the lettuce, feta, basil, the remaining garlic, and 1 tablespoon of the olive oil, tossing to combine.

4. Heat 1 tablespoon of the olive oil in a skillet over medium-high heat. Add the broccoli and cook for 2 minutes, or until softened. Turn the heat off, place a lid on the skillet, and let the broccoli sit for 5 minutes, then transfer the broccoli to a bowl.

5. Heat the remaining 1 tablespoon of olive oil in the now-empty skillet over medium-high heat. Add the salmon and cook for 3–4 minutes per side, until golden.

6. Divide the cabbage and lettuce mixture between two serving bowls. Top with the broccoli, salmon, olives, and hummus. Serve and enjoy!

| NUTRITION · per one serving · % of Daily Value | | | | | |
|---|---|---|---|---|---|
| Calories | 386 | | Dietary Fiber | 3 g | 12% |
| Total Fat | 26.2 g | 40% | Total Sugars | 3 g | — |
| Saturated Fat | 6 g | 30% | Protein | 28.7 g | 57% |
| Polyunsaturated Fat | 3 g | — | Vitamin A | 512 mcg | 47% |
| Monounsaturated Fat | 14 g | — | Vitamin C | 27.9 mcg | 47% |
| Trans Fat | 0.045 g | — | Vitamin D | 12 mcg | 83% |
| Cholesterol | 69 mg | 18% | Potassium | 690 mg | 15% |
| Sodium | 521 mg | 22% | Calcium | 186 mg | 19% |
| Total Carbohydrates | 9.8 g | 23% | Iron | 2.73 mg | 15% |

# Vegan Chickpea & Tahini Wraps

**Servings: 4**

**PREP TIME:** 10 minutes | **COOK TIME:** 5 minutes | **TOTAL TIME:** 15 minutes

Level 3: Moderate

Chickpeas are such a versatile ingredient. They adapt to the flavor of their seasonings and add a boost of plant-based protein to any *meal*. Serve these wraps for a light dinner or pair them with Sage Baked Salmon (page 125) or Italian Chicken (page 232) if you're feeling ravenous!

## INGREDIENTS:

- 1 tablespoon extra-virgin olive oil
- 1 cup canned chickpeas, drained and rinsed
- 2 garlic cloves, minced, divided
- 1 teaspoon crushed red pepper flakes
- ½ teaspoon dried mint
- 1½ tablespoons tahini
- 1 tablespoon lemon juice
- 1 tablespoon water
- 4 (6-inch) whole-wheat tortillas
- ½ cup hummus
- ½ cup spinach
- 1 medium tomato, sliced
- 1 medium cucumber, sliced

## INSTRUCTIONS:

1. Heat the olive oil in a skillet over medium-high heat. Add the chickpeas and cook for 2 minutes, stirring occasionally. Stir in half the garlic, the crushed red pepper, and mint, and cook for 1 minute more, then remove from the heat.

2. Whisk together the tahini, lemon juice, water, and remaining garlic in a small bowl until creamy.

3. Arrange the tortillas on serving plates and smear each with 2 tablespoons of hummus. Place a handful of spinach in the center of each tortilla, then add 3 tablespoons of the chickpea mixture and top with tomato and cucumber slices. Finish with a heaping tablespoon of the tahini sauce.

4. Roll each wrap up like a burrito and serve!

| NUTRITION · per one serving · % of Daily Value | | | | | |
|---|---|---|---|---|---|
| Calories | 413 | | Dietary Fiber | 9 g | 35% |
| Total Fat | 12.6 g | 20% | Total Sugars | 9 g | — |
| Saturated Fat | 1.9 g | 10% | Protein | 15.9 g | 32% |
| Polyunsaturated Fat | 3.7 g | — | Vitamin A | 172 mcg | 14% |
| Monounsaturated Fat | 5.8 g | — | Vitamin C | 12 mcg | 20% |
| *Trans* Fat | — | — | Vitamin D | — | — |
| Cholesterol | — | — | Potassium | 633 mg | 13% |
| Sodium | 367 mg | 15% | Calcium | 132 mg | 13% |
| Total Carbohydrates | 60.7 g | 20% | Iron | 4.6 mg | 26% |

**GF**
**SF**
**EF**

# Italian Chicken Wraps

**Servings: 2**

**PREP TIME:** 10 minutes | **COOK TIME:** 5 minutes | **TOTAL TIME:** 15 minutes

Level 3: Moderate

Tortillas loaded with hearty chicken, creamy mozzarella, grilled zucchini, and zesty pesto. This recipe transforms your typical wrap into an Italian delicacy brimming with vitamins, protein, and calcium. Serve these to your dinner guests and expect compliments to the chef.

## INGREDIENTS:

1 cup chicken, cooked and shredded

2 tablespoons grated Parmesan

2 tablespoons pesto

2 tablespoons tomato paste

2 garlic cloves, minced

½ cup spinach

½ cup sliced grilled zucchini

⅓ cup mozzarella, shredded

2 tablespoons chopped fresh basil

2 tablespoons pitted and chopped olives

2 (8-inch) gluten-free tortillas

## INSTRUCTIONS:

1. Combine the chicken, Parmesan, pesto, tomato paste, and garlic in a bowl, mixing well.

2. Combine the spinach, zucchini, mozzarella, basil, and olives in a separate bowl, tossing to combine.

3. Place the tortillas on separate serving plates and divide the chicken mixture between them, placing it in the center. Top with the spinach mixture and roll each tortilla up like a burrito.

4. Place both wraps in a non-stick skillet over medium-high heat. Toast for 2–3 minutes per side, until golden brown. Remove from the heat.

5. Slice the wraps in half and serve.

| NUTRITION · per one serving · % of Daily Value | | | | | |
|---|---|---|---|---|---|
| Calories | 405 | | Dietary Fiber | 4 g | 12% |
| Total Fat | 15.7 g | 24% | Total Sugars | 3 g | — |
| Saturated Fat | 3.2 g | 16% | Protein | 33.5 g | 67% |
| Polyunsaturated Fat | 2.9 g | — | Vitamin A | 362 mcg | 28% |
| Monounsaturated Fat | 8.4 g | — | Vitamin C | 8.7 mcg | 15% |
| Trans Fat | — | — | Vitamin D | 0.1 mcg | — |
| Cholesterol | 59 mg | 20% | Potassium | 549 mg | 12% |
| Sodium | 749 mg | 33% | Calcium | 357 mg | 36% |
| Total Carbohydrates | 32 g | 11% | Iron | 4.01 mg | 22% |

**NF** **GF** **SF** **EF**

# Greek Cauliflower Chicken Wraps

**Servings: 2**

**PREP TIME:** 10 minutes | **COOK TIME:** 10 minutes | **TOTAL TIME:** 20 minutes

Level 3: Moderate

While most people identify tzatziki as Greek, the sauce is actually a Southern European and Middle Eastern appetizer that originated in the Balkans. It's traditionally served with bread, but here we pair it with gluten-free tortillas, chicken, and veggies for a refreshing meal.

## INGREDIENTS:

2 chicken breasts, grilled and cut into strips, or 3 cups leftover cooked chicken

½ cup tzatziki

2 tablespoons extra-virgin olive oil, divided

1 tablespoon minced fresh mint

1 garlic clove, minced

1 teaspoon ground coriander

½ teaspoon crushed red pepper flakes

1 cup cauliflower florets

2 (6-inch) gluten-free tortillas

1 small onion, chopped

1 small cucumber, chopped

½ cup fresh spinach

½ cup halved cherry tomatoes

2 tablespoons chopped fresh parsley

## INSTRUCTIONS:

1. Combine the chicken, tzatziki, 1 tablespoon of the olive oil, mint, garlic, coriander, and red pepper flakes in a non-stick skillet over medium-high heat. Cook for 3–4 minutes, until the chicken is heated through. Transfer to a heat-safe bowl.

2. Place the remaining 1 tablespoon of olive oil into the skillet and return it to medium-high heat. Add the cauliflower and cook for 3–4 minutes, until tender.

3. Arrange the tortillas on two serving plates and divide the chicken mixture equally between them. Top with the cauliflower, onion, cucumber, spinach, tomatoes, and parsley. Roll up each tortilla like a burrito and serve!

| NUTRITION · per one serving · % of Daily Value | | | | | |
|---|---|---|---|---|---|
| Calories | 462 | | Dietary Fiber | 11 g | 39% |
| Total Fat | 27 g | 35% | Total Sugars | 13 g | — |
| Saturated Fat | 5 g | 25% | Protein | 28 g | 56% |
| Polyunsaturated Fat | 6.7 g | — | Vitamin A | 152 mcg | 15% |
| Monounsaturated Fat | 8.3 g | — | Vitamin C | 8 mcg | 8% |
| Trans Fat | — | — | Vitamin D | 0.2 mcg | — |
| Cholesterol | 86 mg | 28% | Potassium | 137 mg | 2% |
| Sodium | 465 mg | 20% | Calcium | 23.7 mg | 2% |
| Total Carbohydrates | 34 g | 12% | Iron | 5.3 mg | 30% |

# Greek Egg Wrap

**Servings: 1**

**PREP TIME:** 5 minutes | **COOK TIME:** 10 minutes | **TOTAL TIME:** 15 minutes

Level 3: Moderate

Eating eggs for dinner always makes me feel like I'm time traveling—when I was a kid, my parents reserved breakfast-for-dinner for special occasions, and now I do the same. Whether we're celebrating my husband's promotion or my kids' report cards, eggs for dinner are always a hit!

## INGREDIENTS:

2 teaspoons extra-virgin olive oil, divided

2 cups baby spinach

1 teaspoon salt

½ teaspoon ground black pepper

2 large eggs, beaten

1 (8-inch) whole-wheat pita

2 tablespoons chopped sun-dried tomatoes

2 tablespoons crumbled feta cheese

1 red onion, sliced

## INSTRUCTIONS:

1. Heat 1 teaspoon of the olive oil in a non-stick frying pan over medium-high heat. Add the spinach and cook for 4–5 minutes, until it wilts. Add the salt and pepper, mix well, and remove from the heat. Transfer to a heat-safe bowl and set aside.

2. Heat the remaining 1 teaspoon of olive oil in the same frying pan over medium-high heat. Add the eggs and cook for 1 minute, tilting the pan if necessary to allowing the eggs to fully coat the bottom of the pan. Cook for 3–4 minutes, until the edges are golden, then gently lift the omelet from the edges and carefully flip it. Cook for 3–4 minutes more, or until golden on both sides.

3. Arrange the pita on a serving plate and place the omelet in the center. Add the spinach, sun-dried tomatoes, feta, and onions. Roll the pita up like a burrito and slice in half before serving.

| NUTRITION · per one serving · % of Daily Value | | | | | |
|---|---|---|---|---|---|
| Calories | 356 | | Dietary Fiber | 3 g | 11% |
| Total Fat | 21 g | 27% | Total Sugars | 2 g | — |
| Saturated Fat | 5 g | 25% | Protein | 15 g | 30% |
| Polyunsaturated Fat | 3.8 g | — | Vitamin A | 183 mcg | 20% |
| Monounsaturated Fat | 6.1 g | — | Vitamin C | — | — |
| Trans Fat | 0.0054 g | — | Vitamin D | 0.4 mcg | 2% |
| Cholesterol | 328 mg | 110% | Potassium | 121 mg | 2% |
| Sodium | 551 mg | 24% | Calcium | 155 mg | 10% |
| Total Carbohydrates | 24 g | 9% | Iron | 2.6 mg | 15% |

## Spanakopita Skillet

**NF**
**GF**
**SF**
**VE**

**Servings: 4**

**PREP TIME:** 5 minutes | **COOK TIME:** 25 minutes | **TOTAL TIME:** 30 minutes

Level 4: Challenging

Traditional spanakopita is a savory Greek spinach pie. This recipe kicks aside the pastry dough and tosses the delicious ingredients into a skillet topped with eggs—talk about a spin on a classic! Somewhere between a spanakopita and a shakshouka, this one-pan dish is a showstopper.

## INGREDIENTS:

1 teaspoon extra-virgin olive oil

1½ cups thinly sliced yellow onion

1 teaspoon kosher salt, divided

½ cup chopped green onions

1½ pounds spinach

¾ cup crumbled feta cheese, divided

½ cup chopped fresh dill

Juice of 1 lemon

½ teaspoon ground black pepper

4 large eggs

## INSTRUCTIONS:

1. Preheat the oven to 375°F.

2. Heat the olive oil in an oven-safe skillet over medium-high heat.

3. Add the yellow onions and ½ teaspoon of the salt. Cook for 3–5 minutes, until the onions become translucent.

4. Add the green onions and cook, stirring frequently, for 1 minute until soft. Stir in the spinach, ½ cup of the feta, dill, lemon juice, pepper, and the remaining ½ teaspoon salt. Cook for 2 minutes, until the ingredients soften.

5. Make four wells in the spinach mixture and crack an egg into each well.

6. Sprinkle the remaining ¼ cup of feta on top and transfer the skillet to the oven. Bake for 8–13 minutes, until the egg whites are firm and the yolk is cooked to your desired level of doneness.

7. Remove from the oven and allow to cool for 5 minutes before serving. Refrigerate leftovers in an airtight container for up to 3 days.

NUTRITION · per one serving · % of Daily Value

| | | | | | |
|---|---|---|---|---|---|
| Calories | 210 | | Dietary Fiber | 6 g | 21% |
| Total Fat | 13 g | 17% | Total Sugars | 2 g | — |
| Saturated Fat | 6.1 g | 30% | Protein | 17 g | 34% |
| Polyunsaturated Fat | 1.4 g | — | Vitamin A | 6165 mcg | 680% |
| Monounsaturated Fat | 3.9 g | — | Vitamin C | 16 mg | 20% |
| Trans Fat | 0.02 g | — | Vitamin D | 1.1 mcg | 6% |
| Cholesterol | 210 mg | 70% | Potassium | 759 mg | 15% |
| Sodium | 640 mg | 35% | Calcium | 404 mg | 30% |
| Total Carbohydrates | 12 g | 4% | Iron | 4.6 mg | 25% |

NF DF GF SF VG EF

# Broccoli & Tomato Bean Salad

**Servings: 4**

**PREP TIME:** 5 minutes | **COOK TIME:** 25 minutes | **TOTAL TIME:** 30 minutes

Level 3: Moderate

White beans have a high nutrient density, a fairly low calorie count, and a great deal of fiber and protein, which means they may help you maintain a healthy weight. Foods that contain substantial amounts of fiber and protein have been proven to encourage feelings of fullness, reducing the chances that you will overeat. Meanwhile, broccoli is a good source of calcium, phosphorus, zinc, and vitamins K, A, and C, all of which are vital nutrients for maintaining strong, healthy bones.

## INGREDIENTS:

1 tablespoon extra-virgin olive oil

1 medium onion, chopped

3 garlic cloves, minced

1 cup broccoli florets

4 large tomatoes, chopped

1 teaspoon salt

½ teaspoon ground black pepper

2 cups canned cannellini beans, drained and rinsed

## INSTRUCTIONS:

1. Heat the olive oil in a non-stick skillet over medium-high heat. Add the onion and garlic and cook for 5 minutes, until the onions soften. Add the broccoli and cook, stirring occasionally, for 5 more minutes.

2. Add the tomatoes, salt, and pepper and cook for another 5 minutes. Stir in the beans and cook for 5 minutes more, then remove from the heat.

3. Allow to cool for 5 minutes before serving.

| NUTRITION · per one serving · % of Daily Value | | | | | |
|---|---|---|---|---|---|
| Calories | **444** | | Dietary Fiber | 18 g | 72% |
| Total Fat | 8.07 g | 12% | Total Sugars | 7 g | — |
| Saturated Fat | 1.2 g | 6% | Protein | 25.8 g | 52% |
| Polyunsaturated Fat | 1.2 g | — | Vitamin A | 403 mcg | 41% |
| Monounsaturated Fat | 5 g | — | Vitamin C | 44.2 mcg | 74% |
| Trans Fat | — | — | Vitamin D | — | — |
| Cholesterol | — | — | Potassium | 1882 mg | — |
| Sodium | 1165 mg | 49% | Calcium | 256 mg | 26% |
| Total Carbohydrates | 71 g | 24% | Iron | 9.66 mg | 54% |

# Vibrant Vegetable Wraps with Tahini Sauce

**Servings: 4**

**PREP TIME:** 20 minutes | **COOK TIME:** 0 minutes | **TOTAL TIME:** 20 minutes

Level 2: Easy

If you're anything like me, you aim for as much color as possible in your dishes! Not only do they look more appetizing, the colors usually indicate an abundance of nutrients—and this wrap is no exception. Serve with nutty tahini to receive bonus antioxidants and essential Mediterranean-Dieter healthy fats.

## INGREDIENTS:

½ cup tahini

¼ cup lemon juice

2 tablespoons chili sauce

1 garlic clove, minced

4 large lettuce or collard leaves

½ cup hummus

4 carrots, peeled and cut into matchsticks

2 avocados, thickly sliced

½ head red cabbage, shredded

½ cup basil leaves

½ cup mint leaves

## INSTRUCTIONS:

1. Whisk together the tahini, lemon juice, chili sauce, and garlic in a small bowl.

2. Place the lettuce leaves onto separate serving plates and spread 2 tablespoons of hummus onto each leaf. Add the carrots, avocados, red cabbage, basil, and mint. Roll up each lettuce wrap.

3. Serve with the bowl of tahini sauce for dipping!

| NUTRITION · per one serving · % of Daily Value | | | | | |
|---|---|---|---|---|---|
| Calories | 442 | | Dietary Fiber | 16 g | 62% |
| Total Fat | 34.05 g | 52% | Total Sugars | 6 g | — |
| Saturated Fat | 4.8 g | 24% | Protein | 11.17 g | — |
| Polyunsaturated Fat | 9.7 g | — | Vitamin A | 3829 mcg | 259% |
| Monounsaturated Fat | 17.4 g | — | Vitamin C | 43.3 mcg | 72% |
| Trans Fat | — | — | Vitamin D | — | — |
| Cholesterol | — | — | Potassium | 1069 mg | 23% |
| Sodium | 248 mg | 12% | Calcium | 294 mg | 29% |
| Total Carbohydrates | 33.58 g | 11% | Iron | 5.6 mg | 32% |

# Simple Mediterranean Salad

**Servings: 2**

**PREP TIME:** 10 minutes | **COOK TIME:** 0 minutes | **TOTAL TIME:** 10 minutes

Level 2: Easy

Meaty artichoke hearts, protein-packed hard-boiled eggs, salty goat cheese, and sharp olives take romaine lettuce to completely new heights. Serve this recipe alone for a light dinner, serve as a side salad with Chicken Penne (page 234) or Roasted Red Pepper Mac & Cheese (page 242), or top each portion with some Mediterranean Meatballs (page 244).

## INGREDIENTS:

2 cups romaine lettuce

2 hard-boiled eggs, sliced

1 cup sliced artichoke hearts

1 cup roasted red peppers, sliced

¾ cup diced cucumbers

¾ cup crumbled goat cheese

½ cup black olives

2 tablespoons fresh basil, chopped

2 tablespoons extra-virgin olive oil

2 tablespoons red wine vinegar

½ teaspoon dried oregano

½ teaspoon dried basil

½ teaspoon salt

½ teaspoon ground black pepper

## INSTRUCTIONS:

1. Combine the lettuce, hard-boiled eggs, artichoke hearts, roasted red peppers, cucumbers, goat cheese, olives, and basil in a large serving bowl. Toss to mix.

2. Whisk together the olive oil, red wine vinegar, oregano, basil, salt, and pepper in a small bowl, then drizzle the dressing over the salad.

3. Divide between two bowls and serve!

| NUTRITION · per one serving · % of Daily Value | | | | | |
|---|---|---|---|---|---|
| Calories | 526 | | Dietary Fiber | 15 g | 60% |
| Total Fat | 38.3 g | 59% | Total Sugars | 6 g | — |
| Saturated Fat | 12.4 g | 62% | Protein | 24.1 g | 48% |
| Polyunsaturated Fat | 3.2 g | — | Vitamin A | 73.8 mcg | 219% |
| Monounsaturated Fat | 19.5 g | — | Vitamin C | 3160 mcg | 123% |
| Trans Fat | — | — | Vitamin D | 1.4 mcg | 3% |
| Cholesterol | 89 mg | 30% | Potassium | 941 mg | 20% |
| Sodium | 1244 mg | 52% | Calcium | 236 mg | 24% |
| Total Carbohydrates | 25.3 g | 8% | Iron | 7.34 mg | 41% |

# Mediterranean Baked Sweet Potatoes

**Servings: 4**

**PREP TIME:** 5 minutes | **COOK TIME:** 25 minutes | **TOTAL TIME:** 30 minutes

Level 4: Challenging

Sweet potatoes are a treasure trove of nutrients—and a delicious one at that! Perfect for an autumn-harvest meal, sweet potatoes promote gut health, support eyesight, and can support your immune system. And if that's not enough to convince you to try this recipe, the creamy hummus and bright lemon juice will.

## INGREDIENTS:

1 (15-oz.) can chickpeas, drained and rinsed

1 teaspoon extra-virgin olive oil, plus more for the potatoes

½ teaspoon ground coriander

½ teaspoon smoked paprika

4 medium sweet potatoes, rinsed, scrubbed, and halved lengthwise

¼ cup halved cherry tomatoes

¼ cup chopped parsley

Juice of ½ lemon, divided

¼ cup hummus

2 tablespoons water

3 garlic cloves, minced

1 teaspoon dried basil

½ teaspoon salt

## INSTRUCTIONS:

1. Preheat the oven to 400°F and line a baking sheet with parchment paper.

2. Place the chickpeas, olive oil, coriander, and paprika on the prepared baking sheet and toss to combine.

3. Massage the sweet potatoes with olive oil to coat, place them flesh-side down onto the same baking sheet as the chickpeas, and roast for 25 minutes, until the sweet potatoes are tender.

4. Meanwhile, combine the tomatoes, parsley, and 1 teaspoon of the lemon juice in a bowl, mix well, and set aside.

5. Whisk together the hummus, remaining lemon juice, water, garlic, basil, and salt in a separate bowl and set aside.

6. Remove the chickpeas and potatoes from the oven. Transfer the sweet potatoes to a serving platter and mash down their flesh. Spoon the chickpeas and the parsley–tomato mixture into the wells in the sweet potatoes and top with the hummus sauce. Serve and enjoy!

| NUTRITION · per one serving · % of Daily Value | | | | | |
|---|---|---|---|---|---|
| Calories | 249 | | Dietary Fiber | 9 g | 36% |
| Total Fat | 4.5 g | 7% | Total Sugars | 12 g | — |
| Saturated Fat | 0.5 g | 3% | Protein | 7.72 g | 15% |
| Polyunsaturated Fat | 1.19 g | — | Vitamin A | 7200 mcg | 487% |
| Monounsaturated Fat | 1.8 g | — | Vitamin C | 30 mcg | 51% |
| Trans Fat | — | — | Vitamin D | — | — |
| Cholesterol | — | — | Potassium | 525 mg | 11% |
| Sodium | 237 mg | 10% | Calcium | 92 mg | 9% |
| Total Carbohydrates | 46 g | 15% | Iron | 2.53 mg | 14% |

NF
GF
SF
DF
EF

# Chicken & Olive Zoodles

**Servings: 2**

**PREP TIME:** 10 minutes | **COOK TIME:** 15 minutes | **TOTAL TIME:** 25 minutes

Level 3: Moderate

Zoodles—zucchini *noodles*—are an easy gluten-free substitute for pasta, and as an added bonus, they take less time to cook! Brimming with vitamins, potassium, and antioxidants, zucchini can improve digestion, aid in weight loss, and improve heart health. Here they're topped with chicken, tomatoes, and olives for a high-protein, low-carb recipe that reheats well for lunch leftovers.

## INGREDIENTS:

4 zucchinis, ends trimmed

1 tablespoon extra-virgin olive oil

1 medium onion, chopped

2 garlic cloves, crushed

2 chicken breasts, cut into strips

½ teaspoon salt

½ teaspoon ground black pepper

¼ cup tomato paste

4 cups finely chopped tomatoes

½ cup cherry tomatoes

2 teaspoons paprika

1 teaspoon ground cumin

1 cup pitted black olives

## INSTRUCTIONS:

1. Run a potato peeler lengthwise over the zucchinis to create ribbons that resemble noodles.

2. Heat the olive oil in a frying pan over medium-high heat. Add the onions and garlic and cook, stirring occasionally, for 5 minutes, until the onions are translucent. Add the chicken, salt, and pepper and cook for 4–5 minutes, until the chicken is golden on all sides.

3. Stir in the tomato paste, then add both the chopped tomatoes and cherry tomatoes. Add the paprika and cumin, stirring to combine. Add the olives and zucchini ribbons and cooking, stirring periodically, for 5 minutes.

4. Remove from the heat and transfer to a serving bowl.

**NUTRITION** · per one serving · % of Daily Value

| | | | | | |
|---|---|---|---|---|---|
| Calories | 664 | | Dietary Fiber | 14 g | 54% |
| Total Fat | 23.06 g | 35% | Total Sugars | 20 g | — |
| Saturated Fat | 3.7 g | 19% | Protein | 71.8 g | 144% |
| Polyunsaturated Fat | 3.2 g | — | Vitamin A | 653 mcg | 60% |
| Monounsaturated Fat | 12.5 g | — | Vitamin C | 58 mcg | 96% |
| *Trans* Fat | — | — | Vitamin D | 0.075 mcg | — |
| Cholesterol | 199 mg | 66% | Potassium | 2721 mg | 58% |
| Sodium | 1644 mg | 69% | Calcium | 264 mg | 26% |
| Total Carbohydrates | 49.2 g | 16% | Iron | 11.14 mg | 62% |

# Mediterranean Shrimp Pizza

**SF** **NF** **EF**

**Servings: 3**

**PREP TIME:** 5 minutes | **COOK TIME:** 10 minutes | **TOTAL TIME:** 15 minutes

Level 3: Moderate

Sometimes all you need is love—and sometimes, all you need is pizza. Thankfully, this recipe is a mix of both! The star of this show is shrimp, but feel free to add whatever combination of leftover produce you have in your fridge. While the ingredients below make for a delicious dinner, whatever you substitute will surely taste just as yummy.

1 (16-inch) whole-wheat pizza crust

1 tablespoons extra-virgin olive oil, divided

1 cup halved cherry tomatoes

½ cup grated Parmesan cheese

½ cup crumbled feta cheese

½ cup chopped sun-dried tomatoes

8 ounces shrimp, peeled and cooked

½ green bell pepper, chopped

1 shallot, thinly sliced

1 teaspoon dried oregano

1 teaspoon crushed red pepper flakes

1 cup arugula

1. Preheat the oven to 375°F and line a round baking sheet with parchment paper.

2. Place the crust onto the prepared baking sheet and brush the crust with 1 tablespoon of the olive oil. Bake for 2 minutes, until the dough is set, but not browned.

3. Remove the crust from the oven and add the cherry tomatoes, Parmesan, feta, sun-dried tomatoes, shrimp, bell pepper, shallot, oregano, and crushed red pepper flakes. Bake for 3–4 minutes, until golden brown.

4. Remove from the oven and add the arugula before slicing. Serve and enjoy!

| NUTRITION · per one serving · % of Daily Value | | | | | |
|---|---|---|---|---|---|
| Calories | 361 | | Dietary Fiber | 2.8 g | 11% |
| Total Fat | 18.49 g | 38% | Total Sugars | 8.28 g | 0% |
| Saturated Fat | 7.67 g | 19% | Protein | 27.52 g | 50% |
| Polyunsaturated Fat | 1.75 g | 0% | Vitamin A | 1072 mcg | 61% |
| Monounsaturated Fat | 7.56 g | 0% | Vitamin C | 31.3 mcg | 41% |
| Trans Fat | 0.35 g | 0% | Vitamin D | 0.086 mcg | 0% |
| Cholesterol | 164 mg | 61% | Potassium | 830 mg | 18% |
| Sodium | 871 mg | 58% | Calcium | 374 mg | 37% |
| Total Carbohydrates | 23.18 g | 9% | Iron | 2.43 mg | 14% |

# Roasted Chicken Thighs with Feta & Kale

**Servings: 3**

**PREP TIME:** 10 minutes | **COOK TIME:** 20 minutes | **TOTAL TIME:** 30 minutes

Level 3: Moderate

These tender chicken thighs wrapped in crispy skin are balanced with briny feta, juicy tomatoes, and steamed kale. Serve this elegant dish with crusty bread or a light salad, such as Balsamic Chickpea Salad (page 112) or Simple Mediterranean Salad (page 168).

## INGREDIENTS:

3 boneless chicken thighs

1 tablespoon Italian seasoning

1 teaspoon garlic powder

½ teaspoon salt

¼ teaspoon pepper

2 tablespoons extra-virgin olive oil, divided

2 garlic cloves, minced

2 cups grape tomatoes

4 cups chopped kale

2 tablespoons crumbled feta cheese

## INSTRUCTIONS:

1. Dry the chicken thighs using paper towels, then season them with the Italian seasoning, garlic powder, salt, and pepper.

2. Heat 1 tablespoon of the olive oil in a skillet over medium-high heat. Add the seasoned chicken thighs and cook for 7–8 minutes per side, until chicken is golden and has reached an internal temperature of 165°F.

3. Transfer the chicken to a plate, cover with aluminum foil, and set aside.

4. Heat the remaining 1 tablespoon of olive oil in the same skillet over high heat and stir in the garlic. Cook for 1 minute, then stir in the tomatoes and cook for 3 minutes, until they soften and release their juices.

5. Stir in the kale and cook for 3 minutes, until it wilts. Transfer the chicken thighs back to the skillet and cook for another minute. Add the feta cheese and remove from the heat.

6. Allow to cool in the skillet for 5 minutes before serving.

| NUTRITION · per one serving · % of Daily Value | | | | | |
|---|---|---|---|---|---|
| Calories | 245 | | Dietary Fiber | 1 g | 4% |
| Total Fat | 13 g | 15% | Total Sugars | 2 g | 0% |
| Saturated Fat | 3 g | 17% | Protein | 24 g | 46% |
| Polyunsaturated Fat | 2.6 g | 0% | Vitamin A | 583 mcg | 52% |
| Monounsaturated Fat | 5.8 g | 0% | Vitamin C | 21.5 mcg | 23% |
| Trans Fat | 0% | 0% | Vitamin D | 0% | 0% |
| Cholesterol | 114 mg | 35% | Potassium | 599 mg | 18% |
| Sodium | 567 mg | 48% | Calcium | 89 mg | 9% |
| Total Carbohydrates | 5 g | 2% | Iron | 2.1 mg | 12% |

# Roasted Veggie Bowl

**Servings: 2**

**PREP TIME:** 10 minutes | **COOK TIME:** 20 minutes | **TOTAL TIME:** 30 minutes

Level 4: Challenging

This colorful bowl features fiber-rich barley and a dynamic herb dressing. I'm a fan of roasting vegetables since it allows them to caramelize and exude a velvety texture. Topped with creamy hummus and avocado, this vegan-friendly dish will surprise the meat-eaters in your family!

## INGREDIENTS:

1 cup water

½ cup dry pearl barley

1 medium zucchini, sliced

½ cup sliced white mushrooms

¼ large sweet onion, diced

10 cherry tomatoes, halved

1 tablespoon extra-virgin olive oil

2 garlic cloves, minced

½ teaspoon rosemary

½ teaspoon dried basil

½ teaspoon dried thyme

¼ teaspoon crushed red pepper flakes

¼ teaspoon salt

¼ teaspoon ground black pepper

2 cups chopped mixed greens

¼ cup hummus

½ medium avocado, sliced

## INSTRUCTIONS:

1. Preheat the oven to 400°F and line a baking sheet with parchment paper.

2. Combine the water and barley in a saucepan set over medium-high heat. When the water boils, decrease the heat to medium-low. Cook, stirring occasionally, for 15–20 minutes, until the barley is tender. Remove from the heat and set aside.

3. Meanwhile, place the zucchini, mushrooms, onion, and tomatoes onto the prepared baking sheet.

4. Whisk together the olive oil, garlic, rosemary, basil, thyme, crushed red pepper, salt, and pepper in a small bowl, then pour the dressing over the vegetables on the baking sheet. Toss to combine.

5. Bake the vegetables for 10 minutes, then stir and bake for another 5 minutes, until tender.

6. Remove the vegetables from the oven and allow to cool for 5 minutes.

7. Divide the mixed greens between two bowls and add the barley and roasted vegetables. Top with hummus and avocado slices, then serve.

**NUTRITION** · per one serving · % of Daily Value

| | | | | | |
|---|---|---|---|---|---|
| Calories | 423 | | Dietary Fiber | 16 g | 64% |
| Total Fat | 17 g | 27% | Total Sugars | 6 g | 4% |
| Saturated Fat | 2.6 g | 13% | Protein | 10.4 g | 21% |
| Polyunsaturated Fat | 2.7 g | 7% | Vitamin A | 642 mcg | 67% |
| Monounsaturated Fat | 11.4 g | 23% | Vitamin C | 36 mcg | 60% |
| *Trans* Fat | 0% | 0% | Vitamin D | 0.025 mcg | 1% |
| Cholesterol | 156 mg | 35% | Potassium | 1090 mg | 23% |
| Sodium | 469 mg | 20% | Calcium | 119 mg | 12% |
| Total Carbohydrates | 59.9 g | 20% | Iron | 4.1 mg | 23% |

# Hearty Pita Tacos

**SF VE EF**

**Servings: 6**

**PREP TIME:** 10 minutes | **COOK TIME:** 15 minutes | **TOTAL TIME:** 25 minutes

Level 3: Moderate

This is a feel-good, fill-you-up meal. Loaded with spiced chicken, tangy sun-dried tomatoes, creamy labneh, and crunchy walnuts, these tacos are an ideal recipe when you're in need of a pick-me-up, and the taco filling is perfect for hearty lunch leftovers. You'll soon forget tacos ever came wrapped in tortillas!

## INGREDIENTS:

1 tablespoon extra-virgin olive oil

½ small onion, diced

3 garlic cloves, minced

1 pound ground chicken breast

1 tablespoon Lebanese za'atar

1 teaspoon ground sumac

1 teaspoon ground cumin

¼ cup sun-dried tomatoes, drained and chopped

1 tablespoon lemon juice

1 teaspoon salt

½ tablespoon ground black pepper

6 (8-inch) whole-wheat pitas

10 ounces labneh

2 cups arugula

1 medium cucumber, sliced

¼ cup chopped toasted walnuts

## INSTRUCTIONS:

1. Heat the olive oil in a non-stick skillet over medium-high heat. Add the onions and cook for 2–3 minutes, until translucent. Add the garlic and cook for 1 minute, until fragrant.

2. Add the chicken, za'atar, sumac, and cumin and cook, using a spoon to break the chicken up into smaller pieces, for 8–10 minutes.

3. Stir in the sun-dried tomatoes and lemon juice and cook for 1 minute. Add the salt and pepper and stir. Remove from the heat.

4. Warm the pita bread in the microwave or a skillet, then arrange the pitas on separate serving plates.

5. Spread the labneh onto the pitas and divide the chicken mixture equally among them.

6. Top with the arugula and cucumber, and garnish each serving with the chopped walnuts. Serve and enjoy! Refrigerate leftovers in an airtight container for up to 3 days.

| NUTRITION · per one serving · % of Daily Value | | | | | |
|---|---|---|---|---|---|
| Calories | 304 | | Dietary Fiber | 2 g | 8% |
| Total Fat | 6 g | 9% | Total Sugars | 2 g | 0% |
| Saturated Fat | 1 g | 6% | Protein | 26 g | 52% |
| Polyunsaturated Fat | 1 g | 1% | Vitamin A | 10 mcg | 2% |
| Monounsaturated Fat | 3 g | 2% | Vitamin C | 7 mcg | 8% |
| Trans Fat | 0.002 g | 0% | Vitamin D | — | — |
| Cholesterol | 51 mg | 17% | Potassium | 502 mg | 14% |
| Sodium | 805 mg | 35% | Calcium | 111 mg | 11% |
| Total Carbohydrates | 35 g | 12% | Iron | 1 mg | 6% |

# Baked Vegetables & Mozzarella

**NF** **GF** **SF** **VE** **EF**

**Servings: 2**

**PREP TIME:** 5 minutes | **COOK TIME:** 25 minutes | **TOTAL TIME:** 30 minutes

Level 3: Moderate

Whoever said vegetarian dishes aren't as delicious as their meat equivalents has clearly never tried this recipe! Few things are more mouth-watering than baked cheese on caramelized vegetables. High in protein and fiber, this meal will keep you feeling full all night long!

## INGREDIENTS:

2 cups cherry tomatoes

1 green bell pepper, sliced

½ cup thinly sliced red onion

½ cup pitted black olives

⅓ cup chopped parsley

3 garlic cloves, sliced

¼ teaspoon salt

¼ teaspoon pepper

3 tablespoons extra-virgin olive oil, divided

6 sprigs fresh thyme

3 sprigs fresh rosemary

8 ounces mozzarella, cut into thick slices

4 whole-wheat baguette slices, toasted

## INSTRUCTIONS:

1. Preheat the oven to 350°F and line a 7-x-10-inch baking sheet with parchment paper.

2. Combine the tomatoes, bell pepper, onion, olives, parsley, garlic, salt, pepper, and 1½ tablespoons of the olive oil in a medium bowl, mixing well. Transfer the mixture to the prepared baking sheet and place the thyme and rosemary on top.

3. Arrange the mozzarella slices on top, then drizzle the remaining 1½ tablespoons of olive oil over the mozzarella.

4. Bake for 25 minutes, until the cheese softens and has a spreadable consistency.

5. Remove from the oven and transfer to a serving dish. Serve with the toasted whole-wheat baguette slices.

| NUTRITION · per one serving · % of Daily Value | | | | | |
|---|---|---|---|---|---|
| Calories | 404 | | Dietary Fiber | 5 g | 21% |
| Total Fat | 26.1 g | 40% | Total Sugars | 10 g | — |
| Saturated Fat | 10.4 g | 52% | Protein | 12.9 g | 26% |
| Polyunsaturated Fat | 2.6 g | 1% | Vitamin A | 351 mcg | 31% |
| Monounsaturated Fat | 11.7 g | — | Vitamin C | 31 mcg | 79% |
| Trans Fat | — | — | Vitamin D | 0.18 mcg | 1% |
| Cholesterol | 50 mg | 17% | Potassium | 517 mg | 11% |
| Sodium | 918 mg | 38% | Calcium | 351 mg | 35% |
| Total Carbohydrates | 32.4 g | 11% | Iron | 3.13 mg | 17% |

# Mediterranean Edamame Salad

**NF GF SF VE EF**

**Servings: 4**

**PREP TIME:** 15 minutes | **COOK TIME:** 15 minutes | **TOTAL TIME:** 30 minutes

Level 2: Easy

If you're unfamiliar with edamame, you've got to try this recipe! While the legume was originally cultivated in China seven thousand years ago, over time it has been incorporated into the Mediterranean cuisine. Edamame is rich in plant-based protein and antioxidants, so it's no wonder it has become a worldwide superfood.

## INGREDIENTS:

1 cup water

½ cup quinoa, rinsed and drained

1 cup frozen edamame, thawed

1 cup fresh spinach leaves

½ cup chopped seeded tomatoes

½ cup chopped red onion

¼ cup crumbled feta cheese, divided

2 tablespoons extra-virgin olive oil

2 tablespoons lemon juice

2 tablespoons torn fresh basil

Zest of 1 lemon

¼ teaspoon salt

¼ teaspoon ground black pepper

## INSTRUCTIONS:

1. Combine the water and quinoa in a saucepan over medium-high heat. Heat, stirring occasionally, until it comes to a boil, then decrease the heat to medium-low and cook for 11 minutes, until the quinoa has absorbed all the water.

2. Stir in the edamame and cook for 4 minutes, until bright green.

3. Transfer the quinoa-and-edamame mixture to a serving bowl. Add the spinach, tomatoes, onion, and 2 tablespoons of the feta cheese and toss to combine.

4. Whisk together the olive oil, lemon juice, basil, lemon zest, salt, and pepper in a small bowl. Pour over the quinoa–edamame mixture, tossing to combine.

5. Sprinkle the remaining 2 tablespoons feta over the salad and serve!

| NUTRITION · per one serving · % of Daily Value | | | | | |
|---|---|---|---|---|---|
| Calories | 237 | | Dietary Fiber | 4.8 g | 18% |
| Total Fat | 11.8 g | 15% | Total Sugars | 4 g | 1% |
| Saturated Fat | 2.1 g | 11% | Protein | 10.6 g | 22% |
| Polyunsaturated Fat | 2 g | — | Vitamin A | 176.3 mcg | 20% |
| Monounsaturated Fat | 6.3 g | — | Vitamin C | 21 mcg | 25% |
| *Trans* Fat | 0.0045 g | — | Vitamin D | 0.8 mcg | — |
| Cholesterol | 2.5 mg | 1% | Potassium | 320.9 mg | 6% |
| Sodium | 275.9 mg | 12% | Calcium | 108.3 mg | 8% |
| Total Carbohydrates | 23.3 g | 8% | Iron | 2.3 mg | 15% |

# One-Skillet Greek Chicken

**Servings: 4**

**PREP TIME:** 10 minutes | **COOK TIME:** 20 minutes | **TOTAL TIME:** 30 minutes

Level 4: Challenging

One-skillet dinners are a favorite in my household. I usually prepare the ingredients a day before to make it even easier on my future self. This specific recipe is one my grandmother taught me years ago when I first visited her in Greece—and with her permission, I'm sharing it with you!

4 large boneless, skinless chicken breasts, split horizontally

2 tablespoons salt

2 teaspoons ground black pepper, divided

7 tablespoons extra-virgin olive oil, divided

2 garlic cloves, crushed

1 cup sliced mushrooms

½ cup chicken stock

½ cup dry white wine

⅓ cup black olives

2 tablespoons capers

2 tablespoons chopped fresh oregano

2 tablespoons chopped fresh chives

Juice of 1 large lemon

⅓ cup crumbled feta cheese

1. Generously sprinkle the chicken breast with the salt and pepper.

2. Heat 3 tablespoons of the olive oil in a skillet over medium-high heat.

3. Transfer the chicken breasts to the skillet and sear for 3 minutes per side, until tender. Remove from the skillet, transfer to a heat-safe plate, and cover with foil or a lid.

4. Add the remaining 4 tablespoons of olive oil and the garlic to the same pan, still set over medium-high heat, and cook for 1 minute, until the garlic is fragrant.

5. Stir in the mushrooms, chicken stock, and white wine and cook for 5–8 minutes, until the liquid has decreased by half.

6. Transfer the chicken breast back to the skillet and add the olives, capers, oregano, chives, remaining 2 teaspoons pepper, and the lemon juice.

7. Cook for 3–4 minutes, stirring occasionally, until everything is heated through.

8. Stir in the feta and cook it for another minute.

9. Remove from the heat and let cool in the pan for 5 minutes, then transfer to a serving platter. Serve and enjoy!

**NUTRITION** · per one serving · % of Daily Value

| | | | | | |
|---|---|---|---|---|---|
| Calories | 531 | | Dietary Fiber | 3 g | 11% |
| Total Fat | 20 g | 26% | Total Sugars | 10 g | 15% |
| Saturated Fat | 12 g | 60% | Protein | 42 g | 84% |
| Polyunsaturated Fat | 4 g | — | Vitamin A | 348 mcg | 40% |
| Monounsaturated Fat | 1 g | — | Vitamin C | 23 mcg | 25% |
| Trans Fat | — | — | Vitamin D | 1 mcg | 4% |
| Cholesterol | 144 mg | 48% | Potassium | 295 mg | 6% |
| Sodium | 546 mg | 24% | Calcium | 68.3 mg | 6% |
| Total Carbohydrates | 18 g | 7% | Iron | 3.1 mg | 15% |

# Gluten-Free Mediterranean Pasta

NF
DF
GF
SF
VG
EF

**Servings: 6**

**PREP TIME:** 5 minutes | **COOK TIME:** 25 minutes | **TOTAL TIME:** 30 minutes

Level 3: Moderate

This recipe is made from pantry staples, making it perfect for using up what you already have in your kitchen! Loaded with nutrients, this gluten-free riff on a classic dish will lighten your mood and fill your stomach. To keep it gluten-free, use brown rice, chickpea, or gluten-free pasta—I'll admit, the protein-packed chickpea option is my favorite!

## INGREDIENTS:

2 tablespoons extra-virgin olive oil

1 onion, diced

6 garlic cloves, minced

8 cups water

16 ounces gluten-free pasta

1 (15-oz.) can crushed tomatoes

1 (6-oz.) can tomato paste

1 cup sliced mushrooms

½ cup chopped Kalamata olives

½ cup chopped roasted red peppers

2 tablespoons chopped fresh basil

1 teaspoon dried oregano

1 teaspoon salt

½ teaspoon ground black pepper

## INSTRUCTIONS:

1. Heat the olive oil in a deep non-stick skillet over medium-high heat. Add the onion and garlic and cook for 5–6 minutes, until the onions are translucent.

2. Stir in the water, pasta, crushed tomatoes, tomato paste, mushrooms, olives, roasted red peppers, basil, oregano, salt, and pepper. Bring to a boil, then decrease the heat to medium-low and cook, stirring constantly, for 20 minutes, until the pasta is cooked to your desired doneness.

3. Remove from the heat and allow to cool for 3 minutes before serving.

**NUTRITION** · per one serving · % of Daily Value

| | | | | | |
|---|---|---|---|---|---|
| Calories | 329 | | Dietary Fiber | 4 g | 14% |
| Total Fat | 7 g | 9% | Total Sugars | 6 g | 8% |
| Saturated Fat | 1 g | 5% | Protein | 4 g | 8% |
| Polyunsaturated Fat | 1.7 g | — | Vitamin A | 152 mcg | 15% |
| Monounsaturated Fat | 4.1 g | — | Vitamin C | 16 mcg | 20% |
| *Trans* Fat | 0.001 g | — | Vitamin D | — | — |
| Cholesterol | — | — | Potassium | 522 mg | 10% |
| Sodium | 941 mg | 41% | Calcium | 49 mg | 4% |
| Total Carbohydrates | 15 g | 5% | Iron | 2 mg | 10% |

**NF**
**SF**
**EF**

# Creamy Spinach & Chicken Pasta

**Servings: 4**

**PREP TIME:** 5 minutes | **COOK TIME:** 20 minutes | **TOTAL TIME:** 25 minutes

Level 3: Moderate

In need of comfort food? This is the recipe for you! Not only will the decadent, alfredo-like sauce lift your spirits, the spinach and whole-wheat pasta are both rich in fiber to keep you full and satisfied. With some broccoli added for crunch and roasted red peppers for depth, this dish will soon become a part of your weekly repertoire.

## INGREDIENTS:

1 pound chicken breast, sliced into cutlets

2 teaspoon salt, divided

1 teaspoon ground black pepper, divided

2 tablespoons extra-virgin olive oil, divided

1 onion, diced

1 cup broccoli florets

12 ounces roasted red peppers, finely diced

4 garlic cloves, minced

2½ cups chicken stock

7 ounces cream cheese

2 cups fresh baby spinach

2 cups whole-wheat pasta

## INSTRUCTIONS:

1. Season the chicken breast generously with salt and pepper.

2. Heat 1 tablespoon of the olive oil in a non-stick skillet over medium-high heat.

3. Add the chicken and cook for 5–8 minutes, until browned on all sides. Transfer the chicken to a plate and cover with aluminum foil to keep warm.

4. Add the remaining 1 tablespoon of olive oil and the onions to the skillet and cook for 4–5 minutes, until the onions become translucent.

5. Stir in the broccoli, roasted red peppers, garlic, remaining 1 teaspoon salt, and remaining ½ teaspoon pepper and cook for 2 minutes, until tender.

6. Add the chicken stock and cream cheese and stir until smooth. Cook, stirring occasionally, for 7 minutes, until the sauce has reduced.

7. Stir in the spinach and cook for 2 minutes, until the spinach wilts.

8. Return the chicken breast to the skillet and cook for 2 minutes, until the chicken is heated through.

9. Divide the cooked pasta among four bowls. Top each portion with the chicken and creamy sauce. Refrigerate leftovers in an airtight container for up to 3 days.

| NUTRITION · per one serving · % of Daily Value | | | | | |
|---|---|---|---|---|---|
| Calories | 484 | | Dietary Fiber | 2 g | 8% |
| Total Fat | 22 g | 34% | Total Sugars | 5 g | 4% |
| Saturated Fat | 8 g | 59% | Protein | 36 g | 72% |
| Polyunsaturated Fat | 7.1 g | — | Vitamin A | 523 mcg | 51% |
| Monounsaturated Fat | 2.6 g | — | Vitamin C | 43 mcg | 54% |
| Trans Fat | 0.003 g | — | Vitamin D | — | 0% |
| Cholesterol | 123 mg | 41% | Potassium | 862 mg | 25% |
| Sodium | 2530 mg | 78% | Calcium | 135 mg | 14% |
| Total Carbohydrates | 33 g | 11% | Iron | 2.7 mg | 15% |

# Simple Sage & Olive Cod

**NF** **DF** **GF** **SF** **EF**

**Servings: 4**

**PREP TIME:** 5 minutes | **COOK TIME:** 15 minutes | **TOTAL TIME:** 20 minutes

Level 4: Challenging

Serve this at your next gathering and expect a round of applause. While most people tend to reserve sage for holiday cooking, I find it's just too wonderful of an herb to use only once a year. Here we pair it with sweet cod and bright lemon for a dish that will instantly impress your dinner guests.

## INGREDIENTS:

2 cups halved grape tomatoes

¼ cup sliced olives

2 garlic cloves, minced

Zest of 1 lemon

2 tablespoons lemon juice

1 tablespoon extra-virgin olive oil

1 teaspoon salt, divided

½ teaspoon ground black pepper, divided

4 (4-oz.) cod fillets

1 teaspoon dried sage

## INSTRUCTIONS:

1. Preheat the oven to 350°F.

2. Combine the tomatoes, olives, garlic, lemon zest, lemon juice, olive oil, 1 teaspoon of salt, and ½ teaspoon of pepper in a medium bowl.

3. Pat the cod fillets dry with a paper towel, then generously season with the remaining salt and pepper. Sprinkle the sage on top. Massage the seasonings into the fillets.

4. Arrange four sheets of parchment paper on a flat surface, like a counter. Divide the tomato mixture among the parchment sheets and top each mound of tomatoes with a cod fillet.

5. Fold the parchment paper's edges over the fillets to seal the fish inside.

6. Place the parchment packets onto a baking sheet and bake for 12 minutes. Carefully open one packet to check the doneness—when ready, the fish should flake easily with a fork.

7. Remove from the oven and allow the fish to rest for 10 minutes before serving. Refrigerate leftovers in an airtight container for up to 3 days.

| NUTRITION · per one serving · % of Daily Value | | | | | |
| --- | --- | --- | --- | --- | --- |
| Calories | 153 | | Dietary Fiber | 1 g | 4% |
| Total Fat | 6 g | 8% | Total Sugars | 2 g | – |
| Saturated Fat | 1 g | 5% | Protein | 21 g | 42% |
| Polyunsaturated Fat | 3.4 g | – | Vitamin A | 172 mcg | 20% |
| Monounsaturated Fat | 0.52 g | – | Vitamin C | 15 mcg | 15% |
| Trans Fat | – | – | Vitamin D | 0.6 mcg | 4% |
| Cholesterol | 49 mg | 17% | Potassium | 645 mg | 15% |
| Sodium | 197 mg | 9% | Calcium | 33 mg | 2% |
| Total Carbohydrates | 4 g | 1% | Iron | 1 mg | 6% |

NF
DF
GF
SF
EF

# Provençal Chicken with Olives & Tomatoes

**Servings: 5**

**PREP TIME:** 5 minutes | **COOK TIME:** 25 minutes | **TOTAL TIME:** 30 minutes

Level 3: Moderate

Provence is a small region in southeastern France that borders the Mediterranean Sea. Its cuisine involves olives, garlic, olive oil, and tomatoes, thanks to the warm, dry climate. This recipe was inspired by my recent trip there and is best served alongside some greens, such as the Berry & Burrata Summer Salad (page 78).

## INGREDIENTS:

1½ tablespoons extra-virgin olive oil, divided

1½ pounds chicken tenderloins

1 medium red onion, chopped

1 teaspoon minced garlic

1 (15-oz.) can crushed tomatoes

½ cup sliced black olives

1 tablespoon fresh oregano

1 cup halved yellow cherry tomatoes

1 teaspoon salt

½ teaspoon ground black pepper

## INSTRUCTIONS:

1. Heat 1 tablespoon of the olive oil in a skillet over medium-high heat.

2. Add the chicken and cook, stirring frequently, for 10 minutes, until browned on all sides. Transfer the chicken to a plate and cover to keep warm.

3. Place the remaining ½ tablespoon of olive oil and the onions in the same skillet and return to medium-high heat. Cook for 3–4 minutes, until the onions become translucent.

4. Stir in the garlic and cook for 1 minute, until fragrant. Stir in the crushed tomatoes, olives, and oregano and cook for 6–8 minutes, until the flavors become incorporated.

5. Return the chicken to the skillet, and add the cherry tomatoes, salt, and pepper. Stir well and remove from the heat.

6. Allow to cool for 5 minutes before serving. Refrigerate leftovers in an airtight container for up to 3 days.

| NUTRITION · per one serving · % of Daily Value | | | | | |
|---|---|---|---|---|---|
| Calories | 384 | | Dietary Fiber | 2 g | 7% |
| Total Fat | 26 g | 33% | Total Sugars | 5 g | — |
| Saturated Fat | 6 g | 30% | Protein | 27 g | 54% |
| Polyunsaturated Fat | 8.7 g | — | Vitamin A | 93 mcg | 10% |
| Monounsaturated Fat | 10.9 g | — | Vitamin C | 18 mcg | 20% |
| Trans Fat | — | — | Vitamin D | 0.3 mcg | 2% |
| Cholesterol | 102 mg | 33% | Potassium | 595 mg | 15% |
| Sodium | 418 mg | 18% | Calcium | 58 mg | 6% |
| Total Carbohydrates | 9 g | 3% | Iron | 2.6 mg | 15% |

**SF** **EF** **DF** **VG**

# Sicilian Spinach & Ricotta Ravioli

**Servings: 4**

**PREP TIME:** 5 minutes | **COOK TIME:** 10 minutes | **TOTAL TIME:** 15 minutes

Level 3: Moderate

All leafy greens are notoriously nutritious, but I just love the versatility of spinach. Toss it into any dish and you instantly increase your fiber, vitamin A, and iron intake—all while increasing blood circulation, reducing blood pressure, and boosting eyesight. You won't be able to stop at just one bite of this healthful ravioli!

## INGREDIENTS:

14 ounces spinach–ricotta ravioli

2 tablespoons extra-virgin olive oil, divided

1 (15-oz.) can cannellini beans, rinsed and drained

1 (15-oz.) can artichoke hearts, quartered

½ cup drained sun-dried tomatoes packed in oil

½ cup pitted and sliced olives

¼ cup chopped fresh basil

3 tablespoons toasted pine nuts

## INSTRUCTIONS:

1. Cook the ravioli in a pot of salted boiling water according to the package directions.

2. While cooking the ravioli, heat 1 tablespoon of olive oil in a non-stick skillet over medium-high heat. Add the beans and artichokes and cook for 2–3 minutes, until everything is heated.

3. Drain the ravioli and transfer back to the pot. Toss with the remaining 1 tablespoon of olive oil, then add the ravioli to the skillet.

4. Add the sun-dried tomatoes, olives, basil, and pine nuts and cook, stirring occasionally, for 2 minutes, until thoroughly heated.

5. Remove from the heat and serve!

| NUTRITION · per one serving · % of Daily Value | | | | | |
|---|---|---|---|---|---|
| Calories | 454 | | Dietary Fiber | 13 g | 46% |
| Total Fat | 19.2 g | 24% | Total Sugars | 1.8 g | — |
| Saturated Fat | 3.9 g | 20% | Protein | 15 g | 30% |
| Polyunsaturated Fat | 11.6 g | — | Vitamin A | 373.5 mcg | 40% |
| Monounsaturated Fat | 4.1 g | — | Vitamin C | 21 mcg | 25% |
| Trans Fat | 0.004 g | — | Vitamin D | 0.2 mcg | — |
| Cholesterol | 20 mg | 7% | Potassium | 470 mg | 10% |
| Sodium | 699 mg | 30% | Calcium | 136.9 mg | 10% |
| Total Carbohydrates | 60.9 g | 22% | Iron | 2.7 mg | 15% |

NF
GF
SF
VE
EF

# Creamy Roasted Pepper Soup

**Servings: 2**

**PREP TIME:** 5 minutes | **COOK TIME:** 10 minutes | **TOTAL TIME:** 15 minutes

Level 3: Moderate

Who knew such a delectably comforting soup could be made with just four ingredients in only fifteen minutes? The soup has a velvety texture thanks to the cream and chickpeas, and in a single serving, you'll receive 80 percent of your daily fiber and 44 percent of your daily protein.

## INGREDIENTS:

32 ounces roasted red peppers

½ cup heavy cream

3 cups baby spinach

1 (15-oz.) can chickpeas, drained and rinsed

## INSTRUCTIONS:

1. Combine the roasted red peppers and heavy cream in a saucepan over medium-high heat and cook for 5 minutes, until simmering.

2. Remove from the heat and allow to cool for 5 minutes, then transfer to a blender. Blend until smooth, transfer the mixture back to the pot, and return to medium-high heat.

3. Add the spinach and chickpeas and cook for 2 minutes, until the spinach wilts.

4. Remove from the heat and divide between two serving bowls.

| NUTRITION · per one serving · % of Daily Value | | | | | |
|---|---|---|---|---|---|
| Calories | 521 | | Dietary Fiber | 20 g | 80% |
| Total Fat | 18.56 g | 29% | Total Sugars | 30 g | — |
| Saturated Fat | 7.8 g | 39% | Protein | 22 g | 44% |
| Polyunsaturated Fat | 3 g | — | Vitamin A | 3719 mcg | 346% |
| Monounsaturated Fat | 4.4 g | — | Vitamin C | 103 mcg | 105% |
| Trans Fat | — | — | Vitamin D | 0.2 mcg | 1% |
| Cholesterol | 40 mg | 13% | Potassium | 1345 mg | 29% |
| Sodium | 1662 mg | 69% | Calcium | 239 mg | 24% |
| Total Carbohydrates | 79.4 g | 26% | Iron | 5.6 mg | 31% |

# Shrimp Zoodles

**NF**
**GF**
**SF**
**EF**

**Servings: 4**

**PREP TIME:** 10 minutes | **COOK TIME:** 10 minutes | **TOTAL TIME:** 20 minutes

Level 3: Moderate

Summer is produce primetime. If you've got a few zucchinis ready for harvest, this recipe is the perfect solution! Creamy, seasoned zoodles topped with golden shrimp and a spritz of bright lemon is an ideal meal to fill up on antioxidants, protein, and endless vitamins.

2 tablespoons
extra-virgin olive oil

1½ pounds shrimp,
peeled and deveined

Salt

Ground black pepper

4 garlic cloves, minced

¼ cup white wine

2 tablespoons unsalted
butter or ghee

Juice of 1 lemon

Zest 1 lemon

Pinch of red pepper
flakes

4 medium zucchinis,
spiralized

¼ cup chopped parsley

1. Heat the olive oil in a skillet over medium-high heat. Add the shrimp in an even layer and generously sprinkle them with the salt and pepper. Cook for 2 minutes, then turn the shrimp over.

2. Add the garlic and cook for 1 minute, until the garlic is fragrant. Transfer the shrimp and garlic to a plate and set aside.

3. Add the white wine, butter, lemon juice, lemon zest, and red pepper flakes to the skillet and cook, stirring constantly, for 2–3 minutes.

4. Stir in the spiralized zucchini and parsley, tossing to combine with the sauce, and cook for 30 seconds, until the zucchini softens.

5. Return the shrimp and garlic to the skillet and cook for 1 minute, until the shrimp is bright pink.

6. Remove from the heat and serve. Refrigerate leftovers in an airtight container for up to 3 days.

| NUTRITION · per one serving · % of Daily Value | | | | | |
|---|---|---|---|---|---|
| Calories | 269 | | Dietary Fiber | 1 g | 2% |
| Total Fat | 13.5 g | 21% | Total Sugars | 1 g | — |
| Saturated Fat | 4.8 g | 24% | Protein | 35 g | 70% |
| Polyunsaturated Fat | 1.2 g | — | Vitamin A | 89 mcg | 12% |
| Monounsaturated Fat | 6.5 g | — | Vitamin C | 14 mcg | 24% |
| Trans Fat | 0.2 g | — | Vitamin D | 0.1 mcg | — |
| Cholesterol | 289 mg | 96% | Potassium | 569 mg | 12% |
| Sodium | 252 mg | 11% | Calcium | 128 mg | 13% |
| Total Carbohydrates | 3 g | 1% | Iron | 1.43 mg | 8% |

# Ravioli & Vegetable Soup

**Servings: 4**

**PREP TIME:** 5 minutes | **COOK TIME:** 25 minutes | **TOTAL TIME:** 30 minutes

Level 3: Moderate

If you're a pasta fan, this vegetarian soup will blow your mind! A cross between cheese ravioli and tomato soup, it's a super-simple weeknight recipe: The most difficult part of this dish is waiting for it to cool before diving in. If you prefer tortellini instead of ravioli, or just feel like experimenting, try swapping them.

## INGREDIENTS:

1 tablespoon extra-virgin olive oil

2 bell peppers, diced

1 onion, diced

2 garlic cloves, minced

¼ teaspoon crushed red pepper flakes

1 (28-oz.) can crushed tomatoes

1 (16-oz.) can vegetable broth

1½ cups hot water

1 teaspoon dried basil

9 ounces frozen whole-wheat cheese ravioli

2 medium zucchinis, diced

½ teaspoon ground black pepper

## INSTRUCTIONS:

1. Heat the olive oil in a saucepan over medium-high heat. Add the bell peppers, onion, red pepper flakes, and garlic and cook for 2–3 minutes, until the onions soften.

2. Add the tomatoes, broth, water, and basil and bring to a boil.

3. Add the ravioli and cook, stirring occasionally, for 8–9 minutes, then add the zucchini. Return the soup to a boil and cook for an additional 3 minutes, until the zucchini is tender. Season with pepper.

4. Remove from the heat and allow to cool for 5 minutes before serving.

| NUTRITION · per one serving · % of Daily Value | | | | | |
|---|---|---|---|---|---|
| Calories | 261 | | Dietary Fiber | 7 g | 25% |
| Total Fat | 8.3 g | 10% | Total Sugars | 11.8 g | — |
| Saturated Fat | 3 g | 15% | Protein | 10.6 g | 22% |
| Polyunsaturated Fat | 0.8 g | — | Vitamin A | 477 mcg | 50% |
| Monounsaturated Fat | 3.1 g | — | Vitamin C | 24 mcg | 25% |
| Trans Fat | — | — | Vitamin D | 0.4 mcg | 2% |
| Cholesterol | 28.4 mg | 10% | Potassium | 731.9 mg | 15% |
| Sodium | 354.4 mg | 15% | Calcium | 97.4 mg | 8% |
| Total Carbohydrates | 32.6 g | 12% | Iron | 5 mg | 30% |

# Pesto Chicken Salad

**Servings: 6**

**PREP TIME:** 20 minutes | **COOK TIME:** 0 minutes | **TOTAL TIME:** 20 minutes

Level 2: Easy

Swap out the mayonnaise in your typical creamy chicken salad for pesto, and you're in for a mouth-watering, nutritious, meal-worthy salad that will invigorate your evening. If you have the chance, prep this dish the *night* before so the yogurt-pesto dressing has a chance to deeply infuse into the chicken.

## INGREDIENTS:

½ cup plain Greek yogurt

⅓ cup mayonnaise

2 tablespoons minced shallots

2 tablespoons pesto

2 teaspoons lemon juice

½ teaspoon salt

½ teaspoon ground black pepper

3 cups cubed cooked chicken

1 packed cup coarsely chopped arugula

½ cup halved cherry tomatoes

3 tablespoons toasted pine nuts

## INSTRUCTIONS:

1. Whisk together the Greek yogurt, mayonnaise (or pesto), shallots, lemon juice, salt, and pepper in a large serving bowl. Add the chicken, arugula, and cherry tomatoes and toss to combine.

2. Top with the toasted pine nuts and serve! Refrigerate leftovers in an airtight container for up to 3 days.

| NUTRITION · per one serving · % of Daily Value | | | | | |
|---|---|---|---|---|---|
| Calories | 209 | | Dietary Fiber | 0.6 g | 2% |
| Total Fat | 15.7 g | 21% | Total Sugars | 1.5 g | — |
| Saturated Fat | 2.6 g | 13% | Protein | 13 g | 26% |
| Polyunsaturated Fat | — | — | Vitamin A | 35 mcg | 4% |
| Monounsaturated Fat | — | — | Vitamin C | 3.6 mcg | 4% |
| *Trans* Fat | — | — | Vitamin D | — | — |
| Cholesterol | 32.1 mg | 10% | Potassium | 216.9 mg | 4% |
| Sodium | 357.6 mg | 16% | Calcium | 73.4 mg | 7% |
| Total Carbohydrates | 3.4 g | 1% | Iron | 0.9 mg | 4% |

# Lemon & Olive Chicken

**NF**
**GF**
**SF**
**EF**

**Servings: 2**

**PREP TIME:** 10 minutes | **COOK TIME:** 15 minutes | **TOTAL TIME:** 25 minutes

Level 5: Ambitious

This recipe draws inspiration from many Mediterranean cuisines: The chicken is infused with Chardonnay for a French twist, mixed with pimento-stuffed Spanish olives, and livened up with Greek seasonings. This dish pairs well with Greek Quinoa Salad (page 114) and Caprese Salad (page 86).

## INGREDIENTS:

4 boneless, skinless chicken breasts

1 teaspoon dried rosemary

1 teaspoon dried oregano

¼ teaspoon ground cumin

½ teaspoon salt

2 tablespoons extra-virgin olive oil, divided

1 medium red onion, minced

4 garlic cloves, smashed

½ cup chopped pimento-stuffed green Spanish olives

½ cup chopped black olives

¼ cup olive brine

2 tablespoons butter

2 tablespoons fresh rosemary

1 large lemon, sliced

¼ cup Chardonnay or chicken broth

2 tablespoons chopped parsley

## INSTRUCTIONS:

1. Combine the chicken, rosemary, oregano, cumin, and salt in a large bowl, tossing to coat the chicken with the spices. Set aside for 5 minutes.

2. Heat 1 tablespoon of the olive oil in a large skillet over medium-high heat. Add the chicken and sear for 3–5 minutes on each side, until golden brown. Transfer the chicken to a paper towel-lined plate to drain.

3. Heat the remaining 1 tablespoon of olive oil in the same skillet, still over medium-high heat. Add the red onion and garlic and cook for 2–3 minutes, until the onions become translucent.

4. Stir in the green and black olives and cook for 1 minute. Add the olive brine, butter, and rosemary and cook for 1 minute, until the butter melts.

5. Transfer the chicken back to the skillet and stir in the lemon slices. Cook for 2 minutes, then add the Chardonnay. Cook for 2 minutes more, until the chicken is golden.

6. Stir in the parsley and remove from the heat. Allow to cool for 5 minutes before transferring to a serving bowl.

NUTRITION · per one serving · % of Daily Value

| | | | | | |
|---|---|---|---|---|---|
| Calories | 330 | | Dietary Fiber | 6 g | 21% |
| Total Fat | 48 g | 62% | Total Sugars | 4 g | — |
| Saturated Fat | 14 g | 70% | Protein | 77 g | 154% |
| Polyunsaturated Fat | 10.4 g | — | Vitamin A | 381 mcg | 40% |
| Monounsaturated Fat | 18.2 g | — | Vitamin C | 16 mcg | 20% |
| Trans Fat | — | — | Vitamin D | 0.4 mcg | 2% |
| Cholesterol | 110 mg | 37% | Potassium | 827 mg | 20% |
| Sodium | 500 mg | 22% | Calcium | 35 mg | 3% |
| Total Carbohydrates | 18 g | 7% | Iron | 1.2 mg | 6% |

# Chickpea Pesto Wrap

**Servings: 12**

**PREP TIME:** 10 minutes | **COOK TIME:** 0 minutes | **TOTAL TIME:** 10 minutes

Level 2: Easy

This unique chickpea pesto is delicious folded into lettuce wraps, but you can also smear the spread on whatever your heart desires; pita bread, toast, pasta, salads, and more—really, the options are endless! Chock-full of vitamins, these lettuce wraps go well with Roasted Red Pepper Mac & Cheese (page 242) or Italian Chicken (page 232).

## INGREDIENTS:

1 (15-oz.) can chickpeas, drained and rinsed

Handful of arugula

¼ cup chopped walnuts

¼ cup black olives

2 green onions, roughly chopped

1 small tomato, quartered

10 basil leaves

1 garlic clove, peeled

1 tablespoon extra-virgin olive oil

Juice of ½ lemon

12 small lettuce leaves

## INSTRUCTIONS:

1. Combine the chickpeas, arugula, walnuts, olives, green onions, tomato, basil, garlic, olive oil, and lemon juice in a food processor and blend until a paste forms.

2. Arrange the lettuce leaves on a serving platter and top with the chickpea pesto. Serve and enjoy!

| NUTRITION · per one serving · % of Daily Value | | | | | |
|---|---|---|---|---|---|
| Calories | 61 | | Dietary Fiber | 2 g | 7% |
| Total Fat | 3.53 g | 5% | Total Sugars | 1 g | — |
| Saturated Fat | 0.4 g | 2% | Protein | 2.1 g | 4% |
| Polyunsaturated Fat | 1.4 g | — | Vitamin A | 117 mcg | 8% |
| Monounsaturated Fat | 1.3 g | — | Vitamin C | 2.9 mcg | 5% |
| Trans Fat | — | — | Vitamin D | — | — |
| Cholesterol | — | — | Potassium | 87 mg | 2% |
| Sodium | 69 mg | 3% | Calcium | 22 mg | 2% |
| Total Carbohydrates | 6.1 g | 2% | Iron | 0.55 mg | 3% |

# Vegetable Quinoa Risotto (Quinotto)

NF
DF
GF
SF
VG
EF

**Servings: 3**

**PREP TIME:** 10 minutes | **COOK TIME:** 10 minutes | **TOTAL TIME:** 20 minutes

Level 3: Moderate

Risotto is a classic Italian dish invented in the fourteenth century. Here we trade the rice for another Mediterranean favorite—quinoa! Rich in fiber and protein, quinoa adds a chewy texture to this vegan dish. With zucchini, mushrooms, and eggplant, this "quinotto" is a superb choice for a chilly winter evening.

## INGREDIENTS:

2 tablespoons extra-virgin olive oil

2 medium tomatoes, chopped

1 cup cooked quinoa

½ cup chopped eggplant

½ cup chopped zucchini

½ cup sliced mushrooms

⅓ cup canned cannellini beans, drained and rinsed

⅓ cup canned corn, drained

1 cup spinach leaves

2 garlic cloves, minced

4 basil leaves, chopped

## INSTRUCTIONS:

1. Heat the olive oil in a non-stick skillet over medium-high heat. Add the tomatoes and cook for 2–3 minutes, until they soften.

2. Stir in the quinoa, eggplant, zucchini, and mushrooms and cook for 4–5 minutes. Stir in the beans and corn and cook for another 1–2 minutes.

3. Add the spinach, garlic, and basil and cook for 1–2 minutes, until the spinach wilts.

4. Remove from the heat and divide among 3 serving bowls.

| NUTRITION · per one serving · % of Daily Value | | | | | |
|---|---|---|---|---|---|
| Calories | 205 | | Dietary Fiber | 5 g | 18% |
| Total Fat | 10.6 g | 16% | Total Sugars | 5 g | — |
| Saturated Fat | 1.5 g | 7% | Protein | 5.1 g | 6% |
| Polyunsaturated Fat | 1.8 g | — | Vitamin A | 374 mcg | 33% |
| Monounsaturated Fat | 6.9 g | — | Vitamin C | 19 mcg | 33% |
| Trans Fat | 0.004 g | — | Vitamin D | 0.025 mcg | — |
| Cholesterol | — | — | Potassium | 554 mg | 7% |
| Sodium | 112 mg | 5% | Calcium | 48 mg | 5% |
| Total Carbohydrates | 24.7 g | 8% | Iron | 1.99 mg | 11% |

# Italian Mushroom Ragu

**Servings: 4**

**PREP TIME:** 5 minutes | **COOK TIME:** 25 minutes | **TOTAL TIME:** 30 minutes

Level 3: Moderate

Typical ragu recipes are not vegetarian-friendly, but here we use Portobello mushroom caps and their juices as a hearty substitute for the usual meat. This recipe tastes delicious as-is, but you can always serve it with a side of pasta if you're feeling famished.

## INGREDIENTS:

3 tablespoons extra-virgin olive oil

2 shallots, halved lengthwise and thinly sliced

1 teaspoon salt

4 cups roughly chopped Portobello mushroom caps

½ cup vegetable stock

3 tablespoons tomato paste

1 teaspoon balsamic vinegar

1 garlic clove, thinly sliced

2 teaspoons finely chopped fresh rosemary

½ teaspoon crushed red pepper flakes

½ cup grated rennet-free Parmesan cheese

2 tablespoons unsalted butter

## INSTRUCTIONS:

1. Heat the olive oil in a non-stick skillet over medium-high heat. Add the shallots and salt and cook for 2–3 minutes, until the shallots soften.

2. Stir in the mushrooms and cook for 8–10 minutes, until the mushrooms become tender and their juices have evaporated.

3. Add the vegetable stock, vinegar, tomato paste, garlic, rosemary, and red pepper flakes. Cook for 10 minutes.

4. Stir in the Parmesan and butter, then remove from the heat. Serve and enjoy!

| NUTRITION · per one serving · % of Daily Value | | | | | |
|---|---|---|---|---|---|
| Calories | 240 | | Dietary Fiber | 2 g | 7% |
| Total Fat | 20 g | 26% | Total Sugars | 6 g | – |
| Saturated Fat | 7 g | 35% | Protein | 8 g | 16% |
| Polyunsaturated Fat | 2 g | – | Vitamin A | 124 mcg | 15% |
| Monounsaturated Fat | 10 g | – | Vitamin C | 4 mcg | 4% |
| Trans Fat | 1 g | – | Vitamin D | 0.5 mcg | 2% |
| Cholesterol | 24 mg | 8% | Potassium | 599 mg | 15% |
| Sodium | 391 mg | 17% | Calcium | 165 mg | 15% |
| Total Carbohydrates | 10 g | 4% | Iron | 1 mg | 6% |

# Bulgur Mujaddara

**Servings: 3**

**PREP TIME:** 5 minutes | **COOK TIME:** 20 minutes | **TOTAL TIME:** 25 minutes

Level 4: Challenging

Mujaddara is a Levantine dish that consists of lentils, caramelized onions, and some kind of grain, usually rice. This one-skillet recipe takes less than half an hour and features fiber-rich bulgur with all the classic spices. If you're in the mood to follow tradition, pair this with a cucumber-mint yogurt!

## INGREDIENTS:

2 tablespoons extra-virgin olive oil, divided

2 medium onions, chopped

½ cup chopped zucchini

1 garlic clove, minced

1 tablespoon ground black pepper

½ teaspoon ground cumin

½ teaspoon ground coriander

½ teaspoon ground turmeric

½ tablespoon crushed red pepper flakes

⅔ cup hot water

½ cup red lentils, soaked and drained

½ cup coarse bulgur

⅓ cup tomato sauce

1 teaspoon salt

½ cup mint leaves, plus more for serving

## INSTRUCTIONS:

1. Heat 1 tablespoon of the olive oil in a skillet over medium-high heat. Add the onions, zucchini, and garlic and cook for 3 minutes, until the onions soften.

2. Stir in the pepper, cumin, coriander, turmeric, and red pepper flakes and cook for 1 minute, until fragrant. Stir in the water, lentils, bulgur, tomato sauce, and salt. Cover with a lid and cook for 8 minutes.

3. Stir in the mint and cook for 8 minutes more, until the bulgur is tender. Remove from the heat and stir in the remaining 1 tablespoon of olive oil. Allow to cool for 5 minutes.

4. Transfer to a serving bowl and garnish with fresh herbs, if desired.

| NUTRITION · per one serving · % of Daily Value | | | | | |
|---|---|---|---|---|---|
| Calories | 325 | | Dietary Fiber | 13 g | 46% |
| Total Fat | 15 g | 19% | Total Sugars | 10 g | — |
| Saturated Fat | 2 g | 10% | Protein | 10 g | 20% |
| Polyunsaturated Fat | 8.3 g | — | Vitamin A | 148 mcg | 15% |
| Monounsaturated Fat | 3 g | — | Vitamin C | 6 mcg | 6% |
| Trans Fat | — | — | Vitamin D | 0.3 mcg | 2% |
| Cholesterol | — | — | Potassium | 712 mg | 15% |
| Sodium | 616 mg | 27% | Calcium | 40 mg | 4% |
| Total Carbohydrates | 44 g | 16% | Iron | 1.8 mg | 10% |

# Lebanese Lentil Soup

**Servings: 4**

**PREP TIME:** 5 minutes | **COOK TIME:** 25 minutes | **TOTAL TIME:** 30 minutes

Level 3: Moderate

This rich, warming soup never ceases to perk me up on a stormy winter day. Featuring disease-fighting antioxidants, bone-fortifying vitamin K, and digestion-boosting fiber, this nourishing recipe is the epitome of Mediterranean cooking—healthy, yet scrumptious!

## INGREDIENTS:

8 cups cold water

1 cup lentils

3 cups roughly chopped Swiss chard

2 medium potatoes, peeled and diced

1 tablespoon salt

½ teaspoon Lebanese seven-spice blend

½ teaspoon sumac

2 tablespoons extra-virgin olive oil

1 large onion, chopped

1 cup chopped fresh cilantro

2 garlic cloves, chopped

Juice of 1 lemon

## INSTRUCTIONS:

1. Combine the water and lentils in a large saucepan over medium-high heat. Cook for 15 minutes, stirring occasionally.

2. Add the Swiss chard, potatoes, salt, seven-spice, and sumac and cook for 15 minutes, until the potatoes are tender.

3. While the lentils are cooking, heat the olive oil in a skillet over medium heat. Add the onion and cook for 4–5 minutes, until translucent. Add the cilantro and garlic and cook for 1 minute, until tender.

4. Transfer the onion mixture to the pan with the lentils. Stir to combine and add the lemon juice.

5. Remove from the heat and serve! Refrigerate leftovers in an airtight container for up to 3 days.

| NUTRITION · per one serving · % of Daily Value | | | | | |
|---|---|---|---|---|---|
| Calories | 287 | | Dietary Fiber | 9.6 g | 38% |
| Total Fat | 0.89 g | 1% | Total Sugars | 4.6 g | — |
| Saturated Fat | 0.1 g | 1% | Protein | 16 g | 32% |
| Polyunsaturated Fat | 0.3 g | — | Vitamin A | 893 mcg | 101% |
| Monounsaturated Fat | 0.1 g | — | Vitamin C | 54 mcg | 91% |
| Trans Fat | — | — | Vitamin D | — | — |
| Cholesterol | — | — | Potassium | 1159 mg | 25% |
| Sodium | 1927 mg | 80% | Calcium | 132 mg | 13% |
| Total Carbohydrates | 56.9 g | 19% | Iron | 5.57 mg | 31% |

# Tuscan White Bean Pasta

NF
GF
SF
VE
EF

**Servings: 4**

**PREP TIME:** 10 minutes | **COOK TIME:** 10 minutes | **TOTAL TIME:** 20 minutes

Level 3: Moderate

Popular in Italy, cannellini beans hold their shape well, making them the perfect partner for pastas, soups, and salads. Here we draw on Tuscan flavors including tart sun-dried tomatoes, woodsy rosemary, and mellow onions to create a creamy, fiber-rich dinner that everyone in the family will enjoy.

## INGREDIENTS:

2 tablespoons extra-virgin olive oil

1 cup chopped onion

2 (15-oz.) cans cannellini beans, not drained

1 cup chopped dry-packed sun-dried tomatoes

1 cup uncooked vermicelli or gluten-free pasta

3 garlic cloves, chopped

2 teaspoons chopped fresh rosemary

2 tablespoons grated rennet-free Parmesan cheese

1 tablespoon kosher salt

½ teaspoon crushed red pepper flakes

5 cups vegetable broth

1 bunch Tuscan kale, destemmed and chopped

¼ cup heavy cream

## INSTRUCTIONS:

1. Press the sauté function on your electric pressure cooker, then add the olive oil and onion and cook, stirring often, for 2–3 minutes, until the onions soften.

2. Stir in the beans, tomatoes, pasta, garlic, rosemary, Parmesan cheese, salt, red pepper flakes, and broth.

3. Place the lid on the pressure cooker and cook on high for 7 minutes, then use the quick-release function and remove the lid.

4. Stir in the Tuscan kale and heavy cream.

5. Serve and enjoy!

| NUTRITION · per one serving · % of Daily Value | | | | | |
|---|---|---|---|---|---|
| Calories | 301 | | Dietary Fiber | 8 g | 32% |
| Total Fat | 14.62 g | 22% | Total Sugars | 12 g | — |
| Saturated Fat | 4.9 g | 25% | Protein | 8.8 g | 18% |
| Polyunsaturated Fat | 1.8 g | — | Vitamin A | 9344 mcg | 104% |
| Monounsaturated Fat | 6.7 g | — | Vitamin C | 54 mcg | 91% |
| Trans Fat | 0.014 g | — | Vitamin D | 0.1 mcg | 1% |
| Cholesterol | 21 mg | 7% | Potassium | 936 mg | 26% |
| Sodium | 1256 mg | 52% | Calcium | 182 mg | 18% |
| Total Carbohydrates | 38.8 g | 13% | Iron | 4.36 mg | 24% |

# Rice & Bean Stuffed Peppers

**NF**
**GF**
**SF**
**EF**
**VE**

**Servings: 2**

**PREP TIME:** 15 minutes | **COOK TIME:** 15 minutes | **TOTAL TIME:** 30 minutes

Level 5: Ambitious

This is another fabulous vegetarian-friendly meal perfect for your meatless Mondays: juicy peppers stuffed with sweet corn, melty cheese, caramelized onions, and fiber-rich rice. This meal is as satisfying as it is customizable—only have a can of black beans instead of kidney beans? No worries! Swap out the ingredients listed here for what's available in your pantry.

## INGREDIENTS:

2 large sweet red peppers, seeded and halved lengthwise

1 cup canned stewed tomatoes

⅓ cup instant brown rice

2 tablespoons hot water

¾ cup canned kidney beans, drained and rinsed

½ cup canned corn

2 green onions, thinly sliced

⅛ teaspoon crushed red pepper flakes

½ cup shredded mozzarella cheese

1 tablespoon grated rennet-free Parmesan cheese

## INSTRUCTIONS:

1. Place the bell peppers cut side up in a shallow, microwave-safe baking pan, cover with plastic wrap, and microwave on high for 3–4 minutes, until tender. Remove from the microwave and set aside.

2. Combine the stewed tomatoes, rice, and water in a microwave-safe bowl, stirring well. Cover and microwave on high for 5–6 minutes, until the rice is tender. Remove the cover and stir in the kidney beans, corn, green onions, and red pepper flakes. Spoon the rice–bean mixture into the bell peppers.

3. Top with the mozzarella and Parmesan and return to the microwave for 3–4 minutes, until the cheeses melt and the bell peppers are tender.

4. Remove from the microwave and allow to cool for 2 minutes. Transfer two bell pepper halves to each plate and serve.

| NUTRITION · per one serving · % of Daily Value | | | | | |
|---|---|---|---|---|---|
| Calories | 341 | | Dietary Fiber | 11 g | 39% |
| Total Fat | 7 g | 9% | Total Sugars | 16 g | — |
| Saturated Fat | 3 g | 15% | Protein | 19 g | 38% |
| Polyunsaturated Fat | 1 g | — | Vitamin A | 215 mcg | 25% |
| Monounsaturated Fat | 0.7 g | — | Vitamin C | 13.6 mcg | 15% |
| Trans Fat | — | — | Vitamin D | — | — |
| Cholesterol | 19 mg | 7% | Potassium | 398 mg | 8% |
| Sodium | 556 mg | 24% | Calcium | 63.7 mg | 5% |
| Total Carbohydrates | 56 g | 20% | Iron | 3.5 mg | 20% |

NF
DF
GF
EF

# Italian Beef Skewers

**Servings: 4**

**PREP TIME:** 15 minutes | **COOK TIME:** 10 minutes | **TOTAL TIME:** 25 minutes

Level 4: Challenging

This is the perfect meal *for* tailgating season! While I love a good burger every once in a while, I grow tired of them during barbeque season. Since this recipe is simple to whip up, it's a great alternative. Pair these seasoned skewers with the Berry & Burrata Summer Salad (page 78) or Thyme & Carrot Chicken Soup (page 228).

### INGREDIENTS:

½ cup balsamic vinaigrette

1 tablespoon Dijon mustard

1 teaspoon onion powder

1 teaspoon garlic powder

1 teaspoon dried rosemary

1 pound beef steak, cubed

1 pound petite red potatoes, halved

2 cups cherry tomatoes

### INSTRUCTIONS:

1. Preheat the broiler. Soak four wooden skewers in water.

2. Whisk together the balsamic vinaigrette, mustard, onion powder, garlic powder, and rosemary in a large bowl. Set aside ¼ cup of the marinade in a separate small bowl.

3. Place the steak into the large bowl and toss to combine with the marinade.

4. Thread the steak, potatoes, and tomatoes onto the prepared skewers.

5. Arrange the skewers on a baking sheet and place the sheet on the center oven rack, a few inches away from the heat.

6. Broil for 6 minutes, then baste with the reserved marinade and broil for 3 minutes more.

7. Remove from the oven and serve!

**NUTRITION** · per one serving · % of Daily Value

| | | | | | |
|---|---|---|---|---|---|
| Calories | 220 | | Dietary Fiber | 1 g | 4% |
| Total Fat | 7 g | 9% | Total Sugars | 5 g | — |
| Saturated Fat | 2 g | 10% | Protein | 25 g | 50% |
| Polyunsaturated Fat | 1.6 g | — | Vitamin A | — | 0% |
| Monounsaturated Fat | — | — | Vitamin C | 23 mcg | 25% |
| *Trans* Fat | 0.007 g | — | Vitamin D | — | — |
| Cholesterol | 46 mg | 15% | Potassium | 743 mg | 15% |
| Sodium | 288 mg | 13% | Calcium | 31 mg | 2% |
| Total Carbohydrates | 7 g | 3% | Iron | 6.7 mg | 35% |

# Rosemary & Garlic Salmon

**NF**
**DF**
**GF**
**SF**
**EF**

Servings: 4

**PREP TIME:** 10 minutes | **COOK TIME:** 15 minutes | **TOTAL TIME:** 25 minutes

Level 4: Challenging

Rosemary and garlic both have an established history in alternative medicine. Rosemary is thought to help wounds heal faster and lower your risk of infection. Garlic, from the onion family, boosts immune function and reduces blood pressure. If you're feeling ravenous, pair this dish with the Mediterranean Edamame Salad (page 184).

## INGREDIENTS:

4 medium salmon fillets, skin on

2 tablespoons tomato paste

3 garlic cloves, minced

1 tablespoon dried rosemary

2 teaspoons finely diced red chili pepper

1 teaspoon salt

1 teaspoon + ¼ cup extra-virgin olive oil, divided

1 lemon, cut into wedges

## INSTRUCTIONS:

1. Preheat the oven to 400°F and line a baking sheet with parchment paper.

2. Arrange the salmon on the prepared baking sheet with the skin side down.

3. Brush the salmon fillets with a thin layer of tomato paste.

4. Mix the garlic, rosemary, chili pepper, salt, and 1 teaspoon of the olive oil together in a small bowl. Spread the mixture over the fillets, then pour 1 tablespoon of olive oil over each fillet.

5. Bake for 15 minutes, or until your desired level of doneness is met.

6. Remove from the oven and allow to cool for 3 minutes. Garnish with the lemon wedges and serve!

| NUTRITION · per one serving · % of Daily Value | | | | | |
|---|---|---|---|---|---|
| Calories | 431 | | Dietary Fiber | 1 g | 2% |
| Total Fat | 15.2 g | 23% | Total Sugars | 2 g | — |
| Saturated Fat | 2.8 g | 14% | Protein | 65.9 g | 132% |
| Polyunsaturated Fat | 2.7 g | — | Vitamin A | 128 mcg | 13% |
| Monounsaturated Fat | 5.1 g | — | Vitamin C | 34.5 mcg | 58% |
| Trans Fat | 0.1 g | — | Vitamin D | 34.5 mcg | — |
| Cholesterol | 146 mg | 49% | Potassium | 1308 mg | 28% |
| Sodium | 826 mg | 34% | Calcium | 34 mg | 3% |
| Total Carbohydrates | 4.2 g | 1% | Iron | 1.67 mg | 9% |

# Beef & Spinach Stew

NF
DF
GF
SF
EF

**Servings: 2**

**PREP TIME:** 5 minutes | **COOK TIME:** 20 minutes | **TOTAL TIME:** 25 minutes

Level 4: Challenging

Seven-spice blend, well known throughout the Middle East, is made, unsurprisingly, from a blend of seven different spices. The recipe varies depending on the region, but my favorite is the Lebanese version, containing allspice, cinnamon, black pepper, ground cloves, coriander, cumin, and nutmeg. Here we use the blend to enrich a comforting beef and spinach stew.

## INGREDIENTS

1 tablespoon extra-virgin olive oil

1 pound ground beef

2 medium onions, minced

3 garlic cloves, minced

2 teaspoons Lebanese seven-spice blend

1 teaspoon salt

¼ teaspoon crushed red pepper flakes

20 ounces frozen spinach, thawed

½ cup chopped fresh cilantro

3 cups chicken broth

Juice of 1 lemon

1 teaspoon lemon zest

## INSTRUCTIONS:

1. Heat the olive oil in a saucepan set over medium-high heat. Add the ground beef and cook, using a spoon to break the meat into small chunks, for 9–10 minutes, until browned.

2. Add the onions and garlic and cook for 2–3 minutes, until the onions are translucent.

3. Stir in the seven-spice, salt, and red pepper flakes and cook for 2 minutes, until fragrant.

4. Stir in the spinach and cilantro and cook for 2–3 minutes, until the spinach is heated through. Add the chicken broth and cook for 5–7 minutes, until the broth has reduced by half and slightly thickened.

5. Meanwhile, mix together the lemon juice and zest in a small bowl.

6. Remove the stew from the heat and divide between two serving bowls. Top with the lemon mixture and serve.

**NUTRITION** · per one serving · % of Daily Value

| | | | | | |
|---|---|---|---|---|---|
| Calories | 410 | | Dietary Fiber | 5.6 g | 22% |
| Total Fat | 19.2 g | 30% | Total Sugars | 6.5 g | — |
| Saturated Fat | 6.1 g | 31% | Protein | 40.8 g | 82% |
| Polyunsaturated Fat | 1.4 g | — | Vitamin A | 5160 mcg | 345% |
| Monounsaturated Fat | 8.8 g | — | Vitamin C | 17 mcg | 31% |
| *Trans* Fat | 0.4 g | — | Vitamin D | 0.05 mcg | — |
| Cholesterol | 105 mg | 35% | Potassium | 1151 mg | 24% |
| Sodium | 1016 mg | 42% | Calcium | 224 mg | 22% |
| Total Carbohydrates | 19.8 g | 7% | Iron | 6.7 mg | 38% |

# Thyme & Carrot Chicken Soup

**Servings: 4**

**PREP TIME:** 10 minutes | **COOK TIME:** 20 minutes | **TOTAL:** 30 minutes

Level 4: Challenging

This Thyme & Carrot Chicken Soup is the essence of comfort—and health! It's loaded with everything you need to fight a cold: protein, vitamins, antioxidants, and fluids. So serve it during the winter months and feel confident knowing you've fueled your immune system. Pair with crusty bread or Spinach Fritters (page 66) for an even more filling meal.

## INGREDIENTS:

2 tablespoons extra-virgin olive oil

1 leek, halved lengthwise and sliced

4 garlic cloves, minced

4 carrots, peeled and sliced

3 parsnips, peeled and sliced

3 stalks celery, sliced

½ onion, diced

2 boneless, skinless chicken breasts

4 cups low-sodium chicken broth

1 cup water

2 sprigs fresh thyme

2 sprigs fresh tarragon

1 bay leaf

1 teaspoon salt

½ teaspoon ground black pepper

2 tablespoons flat-leaf parsley

## INSTRUCTIONS:

1. Heat the olive oil in a pot or deep skillet over medium-high heat. Add the leek and garlic and cook for 1 minute, until the garlic is fragrant.

2. Stir in the carrots, parsnips, celery, and onion and cook for 3–4 minutes, until the vegetables soften.

3. Add the chicken breasts, chicken broth, water, thyme, tarragon, bay leaf, salt, and pepper and bring to a boil.

4. Decrease the heat to medium-low and cook, stirring occasionally, for 15 minutes.

5. Remove the chicken breasts and shred, then return the shredded chicken to the pot and cook for 2 minutes more.

6. Remove from the heat and discard the thyme and tarragon sprigs and the bay leaf. Divide the soup among four serving bowls and garnish with the parsley.

NUTRITION • per one serving • % of Daily Value

| | | | | | |
|---|---|---|---|---|---|
| Calories | 371 | | Dietary Fiber | 8 g | 29% |
| Total Fat | 12 g | 15% | Total Sugars | 10 g | — |
| Saturated Fat | 2 g | 10% | Protein | 31 g | 62% |
| Polyunsaturated Fat | 9 g | — | Vitamin A | 1770 mcg | 200% |
| Monounsaturated Fat | 0.7 g | — | Vitamin C | 31.6 mcg | 35% |
| Trans Fat | 0.002 g | — | Vitamin D | 0.4 mcg | 2% |
| Cholesterol | 72 mg | 23% | Potassium | 1424 mg | 30% |
| Sodium | 286 mg | 13% | Calcium | 122 mg | 12% |
| Total Carbohydrates | 36 g | 13% | Iron | 2.8 mg | 15% |

# Mackerel & Tomato Spaghetti

**NF**
**DF**
**SF**
**EF**

**Servings: 2**

**PREP TIME:** 10 minutes | **COOK TIME:** 20 minutes | **TOTAL TIME:** 30 minutes

Level 4: Ambitious

Rich in omega-3, mackerel is a common protein source for people from the Mediterranean. You can use fresh or canned, depending on what's more convenient for you. If you choose fresh, note that you'll need to add olive oil, salt, and pepper along with the fish in Step 2.

## INGREDIENTS:

4 ounces whole-wheat spaghetti

2 (4-oz.) cans mackerel packed in oil, or 8 oz. fresh mackerel

2 garlic cloves, minced

2 cups halved cherry tomatoes

1 large red bell pepper, seeded and diced

10 green olives, pitted and roughly chopped

Salt and pepper, to taste

Handful of parsley, chopped

Juice of 1 lemon

## INSTRUCTIONS:

1. Cook the spaghetti in a pot of salted boiling water according to the package directions, then drain and set aside.

2. If using fresh mackerel, combine the fish with 5 tablespoons olive oil, 1 teaspoon salt, and ½ teaspoon ground black pepper in a skillet over medium-high heat. Cook for 10–15 minutes, turning once halfway through, until golden brown. If using canned mackerel, place the mackerel along with its oil in a skillet over medium-high heat.

3. Add the garlic and cook for 2–3 minutes, until golden brown.

4. Add the tomatoes, bell pepper, olives, salt, and pepper and cook for 10 minutes, until the bell peppers and tomatoes are tender.

5. Transfer the spaghetti to the skillet and cook for 1 minute, until the spaghetti is heated through.

6. Remove from heat, garnish with the parsley, and drizzle with the lemon juice before serving.

| NUTRITION · per one serving · % of Daily Value | | | | | |
|---|---|---|---|---|---|
| Calories | 560 | | Dietary Fiber | 7.5 g | 30% |
| Total Fat | 20 g | 36% | Total Sugars | 11.5 g | — |
| Saturated Fat | 4.1 g | 21% | Protein | 22.2 g | 51% |
| Polyunsaturated Fat | 3.1 g | — | Vitamin A | 857 mcg | 83% |
| Monounsaturated Fat | 10.9 g | — | Vitamin C | 140 mcg | 234% |
| Trans Fat | — | — | Vitamin D | 10.55 mcg | 20% |
| Cholesterol | 46 mg | 15% | Potassium | 1030 mg | 22% |
| Sodium | 851 mg | 35% | Calcium | 76 mg | 8% |
| Total Carbohydrates | 71.2 g | 25% | Iron | 3.4 mg | 19% |

# Italian Chicken

**Servings: 4**

**PREP TIME:** 5 minutes | **COOK TIME:** 25 minutes | **TOTAL TIME:** 30 minutes

Level 4: Challenging

Poultry is a popular Mediterranean Diet protein, since it contains nutrients that protect against heart disease, cancer, and diabetes. Here, meaty mushrooms, crisp white wine, and acidic tomatoes give seasoned chicken an Italian makeover. Marry this recipe with Honey Mustard Bean Salad (page 140) for a flavorful feast!

## INGREDIENTS:

2 chicken breasts, halved lengthwise

2 teaspoons salt, divided

2 teaspoons pepper

2 tablespoons extra-virgin olive oil, divided

1 onion, diced

1 (15-oz.) can diced tomatoes, undrained

½ cup sliced mushrooms

3 garlic cloves, minced

½ cup white wine

1 tablespoon lemon juice

1 teaspoon Italian seasoning

½ cup chopped parsley

## INSTRUCTIONS:

1. Generously season the chicken breasts with salt and the pepper.

2. Heat 1 tablespoon of the olive oil in a skillet over medium-high heat. Add the chicken breasts and cook for 2–3 minutes per side, until browned on both sides. Remove from the skillet, transfer to a plate, and cover to keep warm.

3. Add the onions to the skillet over medium-high heat and cook for 3–5 minutes, until they become translucent.

4. Add the tomatoes, mushrooms, garlic, white wine, lemon juice, Italian seasoning, and remaining 1 teaspoon salt and cook, covered, for 15–20 minutes, stirring periodically.

5. Add the parsley and return the chicken to the skillet. Cook for 8–10 minutes, until the chicken has reached an internal temperature of 165°F.

6. Remove from the heat and divide among four serving bowls.

| NUTRITION · per one serving · % of Daily Value | | | | | |
|---|---|---|---|---|---|
| Calories | 292 | | Dietary Fiber | 3 g | 13% |
| Total Fat | 14 g | 22% | Total Sugars | 5 g | — |
| Saturated Fat | 2 g | 13% | Protein | 26 g | 52% |
| Polyunsaturated Fat | 8.1 g | — | Vitamin A | 188 mcg | 19% |
| Monounsaturated Fat | 0.5 g | — | Vitamin C | 26 mcg | 32% |
| *Trans* Fat | — | — | Vitamin D | 0.2 mcg | 1% |
| Cholesterol | 76 mg | 24% | Potassium | 730 mg | 21% |
| Sodium | 1041 mg | 45% | Calcium | 96 mg | 10% |
| Total Carbohydrates | 11 g | 4% | Iron | 2 mg | 11% |

**NF**
**SF**
**EF**

# Chicken Penne

**Servings: 4**

**PREP TIME:** 10 minutes | **COOK TIME:** 20 minutes | **TOTAL TIME:** 30 minutes

Level 5: Ambitious

Penne is the plural form of the Italian word *penna*, meaning "feather" or "pen." The pasta got its name because back when it was invented, its shape resembled a fountain pen's steel nibs. This creamy recipe takes penne to new heights with chicken thighs—which are loaded with iron and zinc, thanks to their higher percentage of dark meat. Serve with garlic bread if you're feeling traditional!

**INGREDIENTS:**

1½ pounds chicken thighs

1 teaspoon Italian seasoning

1 teaspoon salt

¼ teaspoon ground black pepper

¼ cup extra-virgin olive oil, divided

½ onion, chopped

⅔ cup chopped sun-dried tomatoes

4 garlic cloves, minced

3 cups low-sodium chicken broth

8 ounces penne

3 cups fresh spinach

½ cup heavy cream

¼ cup grated Parmesan cheese

2 tablespoons chopped fresh parsley

2 tablespoons lemon juice

**INSTRUCTIONS:**

1. Season the chicken thighs with the Italian seasoning, salt, and pepper.

2. Heat 2 tablespoons of the olive oil in a deep non-stick skillet over medium-high heat. Add the chicken thighs and cook for 3–4 minutes per side, until golden brown.

3. Transfer the chicken thighs to a plate and set aside.

4. Heat the remaining 2 tablespoons olive oil in the same skillet over medium-high heat. Add the onions and cook for 4–5 minutes, until translucent.

5. Stir in the sun-dried tomatoes and garlic and cook for 1 minute, until fragrant.

6. Add the chicken broth and penne and bring to a boil. Cook for 10–12 minutes, then decrease the heat to medium-low and return the chicken thighs to the pot.

7. Cook, covered, for 8–10 minutes or until the pasta is tender, stirring occasionally.

8. Add the spinach, heavy cream, and Parmesan to the skillet, stirring to combine.

9. Remove from the heat and divide among four serving bowls. Garnish with parsley and drizzle with lemon juice, then serve.

| NUTRITION · per one serving · % of Daily Value | | | | | |
|---|---|---|---|---|---|
| Calories | 820 | | Dietary Fiber | 5 g | 21% |
| Total Fat | 54 g | 80% | Total Sugars | 9 g | – |
| Saturated Fat | 16 g | 103% | Protein | 42 g | 84% |
| Polyunsaturated Fat | 14.7 g | – | Vitamin A | 598 mcg | 58% |
| Monounsaturated Fat | 20.1 g | – | Vitamin C | 16 mcg | 19% |
| Trans Fat | 1 g | – | Vitamin D | 0.4 mcg | 2% |
| Cholesterol | 213 mg | 71% | Potassium | 1298 mg | 37% |
| Sodium | 887 mg | 39% | Calcium | 174 mg | 17% |
| Total Carbohydrates | 57 g | 19% | Iron | 5 mg | 28% |

# Moroccan Chicken

**DF**
**GF**
**SF**
**EF**
**NF**

Servings: 4

**PREP TIME:** 5 minutes | **COOK TIME:** 25 minutes | **TOTAL TIME:** 30 minutes

Level 4: Challenging

Moroccans love sweetening their dishes with dried fruits, including dates and apricots. Here the dried fruit enhances the chicken's sauce, balancing the spice from the jalapeño. Topped with almonds for crunch and laid upon a bed of nutty couscous, this chicken is as authentic as it gets!

## INGREDIENTS:

¼ cup all-purpose flour

1 teaspoon salt, divided

⅛ teaspoon ground black pepper

1½ pounds boneless, skinless chicken thighs

1 tablespoon extra-virgin olive oil

1 medium yellow onion, thinly sliced

1 tablespoon minced jalapeño

1 garlic clove, minced

2 teaspoons Moroccan spice

1 cup low-sodium chicken broth

½ cup halved dried dates

½ cup chopped dried apricots

1 (15-oz.) can chickpeas, drained and rinsed

1 teaspoon red wine vinegar

2 cups cooked couscous

2 tablespoons sliced almonds

## INSTRUCTIONS:

1. Whisk the all-purpose flour, ¾ teaspoon of the salt, and the pepper together in a shallow baking dish.

2. Dry the chicken thighs with paper towels and dredge both sides in the seasoned flour.

3. Heat the olive oil in a non-stick skillet over medium-high heat. Add the chicken thighs and cook for 3–4 minutes per side, until golden, then transfer to a plate and set aside.

4. Add the onions to the skillet, still over medium-high heat, and cook for 5–7 minutes, until they are translucent and golden.

5. Add the jalapeño, garlic, and Moroccan spice and cook for 1 minute, until the garlic is fragrant.

6. Stir in the chicken broth, dates, and apricots, then transfer the chicken back to the skillet and decrease the heat to medium-low. Cook, stirring occasionally, for 10 minutes.

7. Add the chickpeas, red wine vinegar, and remaining ¼ teaspoon of salt. Stir well and remove from the heat.

8. Divide the couscous among four serving bowls and top with the Moroccan Chicken. Garnish each serving with the sliced almonds.

| NUTRITION · per one serving · % of Daily Value | | | | | |
|---|---|---|---|---|---|
| Calories | 631 | | Dietary Fiber | 10.46g | 37% |
| Total Fat | 16.02g | 23% | Total Sugars | 30.75g | % |
| Saturated Fat | 2.87 | 14% | Protein | 46.22g | 92% |
| Polyunsaturated Fat | 3.45g | % | Vitamin A | 210mcg | 25% |
| Monounsaturated Fat | 7.33g | % | Vitamin C | 4.15mcg | 5% |
| Trans Fat | 0.03g | % | Vitamin D | 0.04mcg | % |
| Cholesterol | 159.89mg | 53% | Potassium | 1082mg | 31% |
| Sodium | 981mg | 49% | Calcium | 99.72mg | 12% |
| Total Carbohydrates | 73.38g | 30% | Iron | 3.92mg | 28% |

# Baked Salmon with Sage

**Servings: 5**

**PREP TIME:** 10 minutes | **COOK TIME:** 20 minutes | **TOTAL TIME:** 30 minutes

Level 4: Challenging

Sage holds an exalted place in the history of alternative medicine, having been featured in a cure for the plague and used to ward off evil. Its culinary usage dates back to the fourteenth century. Today, sage is a popular herb in Italian cuisine for seasoning fish. Peppery sage contrasts with the savory salmon here to create an appetizing, protein-packed dinner!

## INGREDIENTS:

2½ pounds salmon

1 teaspoon salt

½ teaspoon ground black pepper

2 small lemons, thinly sliced

2 cups halved cherry tomatoes

½ cup artichoke hearts

½ cup olives

¼ red onion, sliced

3 sprigs fresh sage

1 jalapeño, seeded and chopped

2 teaspoons capers

¼ cup extra-virgin olive oil

## INSTRUCTIONS:

1. Preheat the oven to 400°F and line a baking sheet with parchment paper.

2. Season the salmon with the salt and pepper. Arrange the salmon on the prepared baking sheet, tucking the thinner end of the fillet under so it will cook evenly.

3. Layer the lemon slices, tomatoes, artichokes, olives, red onion, sage, jalapeño, and capers on top of and around the salmon. Drizzle the olive oil over the salmon and bake for 20 minutes, until the salmon has a bright pink color and flakes easily with a fork.

4. Remove from the oven and allow to cool for 3 minutes before serving. Refrigerate leftovers in an airtight container for up to 3 days.

**NUTRITION** · per one serving · % of Daily Value

| | | | | | |
|---|---|---|---|---|---|
| Calories | 422 | | Dietary Fiber | 2 g | 7% |
| Total Fat | 27 g | 35% | Total Sugars | 2 g | — |
| Saturated Fat | 6 g | 30% | Protein | 39 g | 78% |
| Polyunsaturated Fat | 6 g | — | Vitamin A | 94 mcg | 10% |
| Monounsaturated Fat | 13 g | — | Vitamin C | 7 mcg | 8% |
| Trans Fat | 1 g | — | Vitamin D | — | — |
| Cholesterol | 114 mg | 38% | Potassium | 1097 mg | 25% |
| Sodium | 317 mg | 14% | Calcium | 46 mg | 4% |
| Total Carbohydrates | 6 g | 2% | Iron | 2 mg | 10% |

# Mediterranean Beef Tacos

**Servings: 12**

**PREP TIME:** 10 minutes | **COOK TIME:** 20 minutes | **TOTAL TIME:** 30 minutes

Level 4: Challenging

This recipe merges Mediterranean and Mexican cuisines with seasoned ground beef enhanced with Mediterranean favorite like olives, sun-dried tomatoes, and roasted bell peppers, then topped with all the classic fixings. As with most of these recipes, you can work with what you've got on hand—pantry loaded with canned beans? Toss them in! Feel free to experiment with the ingredients; with a recipe this delicious, you just can't lose.

- 1 pound 90 percent lean ground beef
- 1 tablespoon chili powder
- 1 teaspoon ground cumin
- ¾ teaspoon salt
- ½ teaspoon dried oregano
- ½ teaspoon garlic powder
- ¼ teaspoon ground black pepper
- ½ cup sliced and pitted green olives
- ¼ cup chopped drained sun-dried tomatoes
- ¼ cup chopped roasted red bell peppers
- ½ cup tomato sauce
- ¼ cup water
- 12 (6-inch) whole-wheat tortillas, warmed
- 1 cup shredded 4-cheese or Mexican blend cheese
- 1 cup shredded lettuce
- 1 small red onion, diced
- 2 tablespoons chopped fresh cilantro

1. Place the ground beef in a large skillet over medium-high heat.

2. Cook for 6–8 minutes, breaking the beef into smaller pieces with a spoon, until there is no pink left.

3. Add the chili powder, cumin, salt, oregano, garlic powder, and pepper, stirring to combine.

4. Add the olives, sun-dried tomatoes, and roasted red bell peppers, stirring to combine, and cook for 2 minutes, until the bell peppers soften.

5. Decrease the heat to medium-low and add the tomato sauce and water. Cook for 7–8 minutes, until some of the liquid has evaporated. Remove from the heat.

6. Arrange the tortillas on a serving platter and add 2 tablespoons of the ground beef mixture to each.

7. Top with the cheese, lettuce, red onion, and cilantro before serving. Refrigerate leftovers in an airtight container for up to 3 days.

**NUTRITION** · per one serving · % of Daily Value

| | | | | | |
|---|---|---|---|---|---|
| Calories | 233 | | Dietary Fiber | 2 g | 8% |
| Total Fat | 7.55 g | 16% | Total Sugars | 2.94 g | – |
| Saturated Fat | 3.122 g | 17% | Protein | 14.61 g | 27% |
| Polyunsaturated Fat | 0.838 g | – | Vitamin A | 568 mcg | 24% |
| Monounsaturated Fat | 2.947 g | – | Vitamin C | 7 mcg | 8% |
| Trans Fat | 0.083 g | – | Vitamin D | 3 mcg | 1% |
| Cholesterol | 32 mg | – | Potassium | 320 mg | 7% |
| Sodium | 561 mg | 37% | Calcium | 136 mg | 14% |
| Total Carbohydrates | 26.81 g | 11% | Iron | 3.04 mg | 17% |

**NF**
**GF**
**SF**
**EF**
**VE**

# Roasted Red Pepper Mac & Cheese

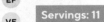Servings: 11

**PREP TIME:** 5 minutes | **COOK TIME:** 20minutes | **TOTAL TIME:** 25 minutes

Level 5: Ambitious

Who knew gluten-free mac & cheese could be so splendid? Thanks to the fiber-rich chickpea pasta in this dish, celiacs can rejoice! Here we elevate the family classic with sweet roasted red peppers, sharp red onion, and fragrant garlic to add vitamin C, vitamin B$_9$, and antioxidants, respectively, to your diet.

## INGREDIENTS:

8 ounces chickpea pasta

2 tablespoons extra-virgin olive oil

¼ cup diced red onion

1 garlic clove, minced

1 tablespoon gluten free flour

½ cup skim milk

1 cup shredded sharp cheddar cheese

1 cup non-fat plain Greek yogurt

1 teaspoon Italian seasoning

½ teaspoon sumac

½ teaspoon ground black pepper

¼ teaspoon salt

1 cup chopped roasted red peppers

¼ cup crumbled feta cheese

## INSTRUCTIONS:

1. Cook the chickpea pasta in a pot of salted, boiling water for 2 minutes less than recommended by the package instructions. Drain and set aside.

2. Meanwhile, heat the olive oil in a deep skillet over medium-high heat. Add the red onion and garlic and cook for 2 minutes, until the onions start to soften.

3. Stir in the gluten free flour and cook, stirring, for 1 minute, until fully incorporated.

4. Stir in the skim milk and cook, whisking constantly, for 5–8 minutes, until it is smooth and thickened.

5. Add ½ cup of the cheddar and stir until it melts, then stir in the remaining ½ cup of cheddar.

6. Add the Greek yogurt, Italian seasoning, sumac, pepper, and salt, and cook, stirring, for 30 seconds, until smooth.

7. Add the roasted red peppers and chickpea pasta and cook for 2 minutes, until heated through.

8. Top with the feta cheese, then serve and enjoy!

| NUTRITION · per one serving · % of Daily Value | | | | | |
|---|---|---|---|---|---|
| Calories | 166 | | Dietary Fiber | 2.98 g | 11% |
| Total Fat | 8.14 g | 12% | Total Sugars | 3.55 g | |
| Saturated Fat | 3.745 g | 15% | Protein | 10.29 g | 21% |
| Polyunsaturated Fat | 0.461 g | — | Vitamin A | 589 mcg | 25% |
| Monounsaturated Fat | 3.0201 g | — | Vitamin C | 22.3 mcg | 30% |
| Trans Fat | 0.123 g | — | Vitamin D | 9 mcg | 2% |
| Cholesterol | 19 mg | 7% | Potassium | 90 mg | 2% |
| Sodium | 224 mg | 15% | Calcium | 140 mg | 18% |
| Total Carbohydrates | 15.02 g | 6% | Iron | 2.26 mg | 16% |

# Mediterranean Meatballs

**Servings: 4**

**PREP TIME:** 10 minutes | **COOK TIME:** 20 minutes | **TOTAL TIME:** 30 minutes

Level 3: Moderate

Make these Mediterranean Meatballs in bulk and freeze them for up to three months to save yourself time and energy on bustling weekdays. These chicken meatballs make a superb lunch dipped in tzatziki, or can be paired with the Broccoli & Tomato Bean Salad (page 164) or the Mediterranean Edamame Salad (page 184) for a simple, satisfying dinner.

## INGREDIENTS:

1 pound ground chicken

½ cup panko breadcrumbs

½ cup crumbled feta cheese

¼ cup minced red onions

¼ cup minced sun-dried tomatoes

¼ cup minced roasted red peppers

1 garlic clove, minced

1 large egg

2 tablespoons extra-virgin olive oil

½ teaspoon salt

½ teaspoon ground black pepper

¼ teaspoon dried basil

¼ teaspoon dried oregano

3 tablespoons plain Greek yogurt

1 tablespoon chopped fresh mint

## INSTRUCTIONS:

1. Preheat the oven to 400°F and line a baking sheet with parchment paper.

2. Combine the ground chicken, breadcrumbs, feta, red onions, sun-dried tomatoes, roasted red peppers, garlic, egg, olive oil, salt, pepper, basil, and oregano in a large bowl, mixing thoroughly.

3. Form the mixture into 15 meatballs, each about 2½ inches in diameter. Place them 1 inch apart on the prepared baking sheet.

4. Bake for 25–30 minutes, until golden brown.

5. Remove from the oven and transfer the meatballs to a serving platter. Top with the Greek yogurt and mint and serve!

| NUTRITION · per one serving · % of Daily Value | | | | | |
|---|---|---|---|---|---|
| Calories | 328 | | Dietary Fiber | 1 g | 4% |
| Total Fat | 21.82 g | 45% | Total Sugars | 2.09 g | — |
| Saturated Fat | 7.043 g | — | Protein | 25.67 g | 47% |
| Polyunsaturated Fat | 2.928 g | — | Vitamin A | 476 mcg | 20% |
| Monounsaturated Fat | 10.503 g | — | Vitamin C | 16.7 mcg | 22% |
| Trans Fat | 0.83 g | — | Vitamin D | 26 mcg | 4% |
| Cholesterol | 162 mg | — | Potassium | 798 mg | 17% |
| Sodium | 590 mg | 39% | Calcium | 141 mg | 14% |
| Total Carbohydrates | 7.92 g | 3% | Iron | 20.2 mg | 11% |

# Greek Salmon Fusilli

**NF**
**SF**
**EF**

**Servings: 10**

**PREP TIME:** 5 minutes | **COOK TIME:** 20 minutes | **TOTAL TIME:** 25 minutes

Level 3: Moderate

With its buttery, smoky flavors, flaky smoked salmon takes pasta to a heavenly level in this Mediterranean dish, tossed with bright red onion, tangy olives, and salty feta. Serve this recipe cold or warm, with soft bread and a light salad on the side.

## INGREDIENTS:

12 ounces fusilli or rotini pasta

1½ cups flaked or cubed smoked or cooked salmon

1 cup halved grape tomatoes

1 cup baby spinach

1 medium cucumber, diced

½ cup sliced and pitted green olives

½ cup sliced and pitted black olives

½ cup crumbled feta cheese

¼ cup thinly sliced red onion

¼ cup thinly sliced red bell pepper

¼ cup thinly sliced yellow bell pepper

½ cup extra-virgin olive oil

½ cup white wine vinegar

2 garlic cloves, minced

2 teaspoons Dijon mustard

2 teaspoons dried basil

2 teaspoons dried thyme

½ teaspoon salt

¼ teaspoon ground black pepper

## INSTRUCTIONS:

1. Cook the pasta in a pot of salted, boiling water according to the package instructions. Drain and rinse with cold water.

2. Combine the cooked pasta, salmon, tomatoes, spinach, cucumber, green olives, black olives, feta, red onion, red bell pepper, and yellow bell pepper in a serving bowl, tossing well.

3. Whisk together the olive oil, white wine vinegar, garlic, mustard, basil, thyme, salt, and pepper in a bowl. Drizzle the dressing over the pasta and toss to combine.

4. Serve and enjoy! Refrigerate leftovers in an airtight container for up to 3 days.

| NUTRITION · per one serving · % of Daily Value | | | | | |
|---|---|---|---|---|---|
| Calories | 240 | | Dietary Fiber | 2.5 g | 10% |
| Total Fat | 15.62 g | 32% | Total Sugars | 1.23 g | — |
| Saturated Fat | 3.15 g | — | Protein | 12.34 g | 23% |
| Polyunsaturated Fat | 1.772 g | — | Vitamin A | 640 mcg | 27% |
| Monounsaturated Fat | 9.509 g | — | Vitamin C | 15.8 mcg | 21% |
| Trans Fat | 0.022 g | — | Vitamin D | 208 mcg | 35% |
| Cholesterol | 29 mg | — | Potassium | 303 mg | 6% |
| Sodium | 289 mg | 19% | Calcium | 62 mg | 6% |
| Total Carbohydrates | 12.49 g | 5% | Iron | 1.04 mg | 6% |

**NF**
**SF**
**EF**
**GF**

# Baked Lemon Salmon

**Servings: 4**

**PREP TIME:** 10 minutes | **COOK TIME:** 15 minutes | **TOTAL TIME:** 25 minutes

Level 3: Moderate

Busy cooks will fall in love with this simple and scrumptious Baked Lemon Salmon recipe! It just takes a bit of prep and the oven does the rest for you. If you're in a time crunch, marinate the fish and slice up your vegetables the night before. And wrap the salmon in foil while baking to spend even less time cleaning up!

## INGREDIENTS:

¼ cup extra-virgin olive oil

Juice of 1 lemon

Zest of 1 lemon

1 teaspoon crushed red pepper flakes

1 teaspoon dried dill

1 teaspoon dried parsley

¼ teaspoon salt

⅛ teaspoon ground black pepper

4 skinless salmon fillets

2 cups halved grape tomatoes

1 cup sliced and pitted green olives

1 cup crumbled feta cheese

½ cucumber, diced

¼ cup diced red onions

¼ cup chopped artichoke hearts

¼ cup chopped fresh cilantro

## INSTRUCTIONS:

1. Preheat the oven to 450°F.

2. Whisk the olive oil, lemon juice, lemon zest, crushed red pepper flakes, dill, parsley, salt, and pepper together in a small bowl.

3. Arrange the salmon fillets in a baking dish and brush them with the lemon mixture. Pour any remaining marinade onto the fillets.

4. Bake for 12–14 minutes, until flaky and tender. Remove from the oven.

5. Combine the tomatoes, olives, feta, cucumber, red onions, artichoke hearts, and cilantro in a medium bowl, mixing well.

6. Arrange the salmon fillets on four serving plates and top each with a spoonful of the tomato mixture. Serve and enjoy!

**NUTRITION** · per one serving · % of Daily Value

| | | | | | |
|---|---|---|---|---|---|
| Calories | 694 | | Dietary Fiber | 1.7 g | 7% |
| Total Fat | 71.84 g | 74% | Total Sugars | 14.61 g | — |
| Saturated Fat | 10.133 g | — | Protein | 71.84 g | 132% |
| Polyunsaturated Fat | 4.304 g | — | Vitamin A | 724 mcg | 31% |
| Monounsaturated Fat | 16.01 g | — | Vitamin C | 15.4 mcg | 21% |
| *Trans* Fat | 0.115 g | — | Vitamin D | 1389 mcg | 232% |
| Cholesterol | 180 mg | — | Potassium | 1445 mg | 31% |
| Sodium | 747 mg | 50% | Calcium | 234 mg | 23% |
| Total Carbohydrates | 19.52 g | 8% | Iron | 2.09 mg | 12% |

# Endnotes

1. Bonaccio, Marialaura, et al. "Mediterranean Diet and Mortality in the Elderly: A Prospective Cohort Study and a Meta-Analysis." *British Journal of Nutrition*, vol. 120, no. 8, 2018: 841–854, https://doi.org/10.1017/S0007114518002179.

2. Estruch, Ramón, et al. "Primary Prevention of Cardiovascular Disease with a Mediterranean Diet." *New England Journal of Medicine*, 4 Apr. 2013, https://www.nejm.org/doi/full/10.1056/NEJMoa1200303.

3. Schwingshackl, Lukas, et al. "Adherence to Mediterranean Diet and Risk of Cancer: An Updated Systematic Review and Meta-Analysis." *Nutrients*, MDPI, 26 Sept. 2017, https://www.ncbi.nlm.nih.gov/pmc/articles/PMC5691680/.

4. Toledo, Estefanía. "Mediterranean Diet and Invasive Breast Cancer Risk." *JAMA Internal Medicine*, JAMA Network, 1 Nov. 2015, https://jamanetwork.com/journals/jamainternalmedicine/fullarticle/2434738.

5. Lassale, Camille, et al. "Healthy Dietary Indices and Risk of Depressive Outcomes: A Systematic Review and Meta-Analysis of Observational Studies." *Nature News*, Nature Publishing Group, 26 Sept. 2018, https://www.nature.com/articles/s41380-018-0237-8.

6. Mancini, J.G., et al. "Systematic Review of the Mediterranean Diet for Long-Term Weight Loss." *The American Journal of Medicine*, U.S. National Library of Medicine, https://pubmed.ncbi.nlm.nih.gov/26721635/.

7. Hardman, Roy J., et al. "Adherence to a Mediterranean-Style Diet and Effects on Cognition in Adults: A Qualitative Evaluation and Systematic Review of Longitudinal and Prospective Trials." Front. Nutr., 22 July 2016, https://www.frontiersin.org/articles/10.3389/fnut.2016.00022/full.

8. Salas-Salvado, Jordi. "Reduction in the Incidence of Type 2 Diabetes with the Mediterranean Diet." *Diabetes Care*, vol. 35, ser. 1: 14–19, https://www.ncbi.nlm.nih.gov/pmc/articles/PMC3005482/pdf/zdc14.pdf.

9. "Nearly 37 Percent of Americans Regularly Eat Fast Food, Study Shows." *Safety and Health Magazine*, 9 Dec. 2020, www.safetyandhealthmagazine.com/articles/17784-nearly-37-percent-of-americans-regularly-eat-fast-food-study-shows.

10. Wein, Harrison. "Risk in Red Meat?" U.S. Department of Health and Human Services, 2 July 2015, www.nih.gov/news-events/nih-research-matters/risk-red-meat.

11. Rico-Campà, Anaïs, et al. "Association between Consumption of Ultra-Processed Foods and All Cause Mortality: SUN Prospective Cohort Study." *BMJ*, 29 May 2019.

12. Folta, Kevin M, and Harry J Klee. "Sensory Sacrifices When We Mass-Produce Mass Produce." *Horticulture Research*, Nature Publishing Group, 13 July 2016, https://www.ncbi.nlm.nih.gov/pmc/articles/PMC4942566/.

13. Johnson, Renee. *The U.S. Trade Situation for Fruit and Vegetable Products*. Congressional Research Service, 1 Dec. 2016, https://sgp.fas.org/crs/misc/RL34468.pdf.

# Index

24215101R00144